P9-DXL-431

634

By the same author

The Elements of Drama
The Dark Comedy
The Dramatic Experience
Shakespeare's Stagecraft
Chekhov in Performance
The Challenge of the Theatre
Drama, Stage and Audience
The Shakespeare Revolution

Modern drama in theory and practice   Volume I

Realism and naturalism

Modern drama in theory and practice

VOLUME 1

Realism and naturalism

J.L.STYAN

Franklyn Bliss Snyder Professor of English Literature
Northwestern University

CAMBRIDGE UNIVERSITY PRESS
Cambridge
London · New York · New Rochelle
Melbourne · Sydney

EGLI Dec/81.

Published by the Press Syndicate of the University of Cambridge
The Pitt Building, Trumpington Street, Cambridge CB2 1RP
32 East 57th Street, New York, NY 10022, USA
296 Beaconsfield Parade, Middle Park, Melbourne 3206, Australia

First published 1981

Printed in Malta by Interprint Ltd

Library of Congress Cataloguing in Publication Data
Styan, J.L.
Modern drama in theory and practice.
Includes bibliographies and index.
CONTENTS: 1. Realism. —2. Symbolism, surrealism,
and the absurd. —3. Expressionism and epic theatre.
1. Drama —History —20th century. 2. Theatre —
History —20th century. I. Title.
PN1861.S76   809.2   79–15947
ISBN 0 521 22737 2 volume 1
ISBN 0 521 22738 0 volume 2.
ISBN 0 521 22739 9 volume 3
ISBN 0 521 23068 3 Set of three volumes

Contents

The dates are usually those of the first production

Contents

Illustrations

Acknowledgements

The author and publisher gratefully acknowledge the permission
of the following to reproduce their illustrations in this book:
Illustrated London News (1); Moscow Art Theatre (2); Teater-
museet, Copenhagen (3); Drottingholms Teatermuseum (4);
Bibliothèque Nationale, Paris (5); Severiges Radio, Sweden (6);
Bildarchiv Preussischer Kulturbesitz, W. Berlin (7 and 8);
British Theatre Museum at the Victoria and Albert Museum,
London (9); Raymond Mitchenson and Joe Mander Theatre
Collection, London (10); Society for Cultural Relations with the
the USSR, London (11, 12, 13 and 14); G.A. Duncan, Dublin
(15, 16 and 17); Hoblitzelle Theatre Arts Library, Humanities
Research Center, University of Texas at Austin (18); New York
Public Library (19, 20, 21, 22, 23, 24, 25, 26, 27, 28, 29 and 30);
Roger Mayne, Dorset (31); Houston Rogers Collection, British
Theatre Museum at the Victoria and Albert Museum, London (32);
David Sim, London (33) and Dominic, London (34).

Preface

It is a principle increasingly accepted that the manner of playwriting is inseparable from the kind of theatre it is written for. The new attempt of this study is to look at some of the important plays of modern times, not as isolated literary works, but in relation to their production and performance. The intention is to trace some of the interactions between playwright and performing artist (this term to include all who are involved in production: actors and directors, lighting and scenic designers), and the subject of the study is, in the widest sense, the bearing of theory on practice, and of practice on theory. Like any art form, drama is sometimes aroused by fitful rebellion, but it always builds upon the testing of ideas on an audience and the total theatre experience of the past.

The story of the theatre is one of rebellion and reaction, with new forms challenging the old, and old forms in turn providing the basis for the new. But the labels we use, realism, symbolism, and so on, too easily blanket the details of dramatic and stage history. These details are not often found in the laws of playwriting or in the manifestoes of fashionable movements, but remain to be extracted from the day-to-day dealings of the stage. We must judge less by intentions than by results, aware that theory and practice are more often in conflict than in accord: in John Gassner's words, we must recognize 'the breach between ambition and attainment'. It is necessary to turn to the promptbook and the acting edition, the *Regiebuch* and the *Modellbuch*, to notices and criticism, interviews and memoirs, as well as to the text of the play itself, to know what happened.

To adapt a concept of the art historian, E. H. Gombrich, drama originates in our reactions to the world, and not in the world itself. By this argument, the changes which an audience perceives on the stage between, say, the grim naturalism of a *Lower Depths* and the violent fantasies of Edward Bond, are changes in itself. The abiding secret of dramatic interpretation lies in its 'style', the *way of seeing* of writer, player or spectator, and style is the one ingredient, it must be supposed, which a play and its performance should ideally have in common, since it is the *sine qua non* of dramatic communication. Moreover, if an artist's perception of reality is conditioned by the age he lives in and by the medium he works with, an understanding of style will supply some of the clues to both. This study, therefore, concerned as it is with the limitations and possibilities of drama since Büchner and Wagner, Zola and Ibsen, may afford an insight into ourselves and our modes of perception.

The threads of many different styles, however, are interwoven within a single play in performance. This is especially true of this century, which can draw upon a multitude of conventions from the 'imaginary museum'. In practice, it is impossible to find a play of, say, naked realism or pure symbolism, and the best playwrights are constantly resourceful: Ibsen is a realist and a symbolist, Strindberg embraces both naturalism and expressionism, in writing a symbolist drama Pirandello becomes a progenitor of the absurd, Weiss arranges Artaudian cruelty within a Brechtian epic frame and so on. Theatre artists are similarly elastic: Meyerhold, the originator of constructivism, produced the outstanding *Government Inspector*, Jouvet showed himself master of Molière as well as of *La Machine infernale*, Barrault produced a fine *Phèdre* and was also superbly sensitive to Chekhov.

A final explanation. In order to follow a clearer path through a jungle of detail, *Modern Drama* is presented as three extended essays on realism, symbolism and expressionism, with developments in the last two into surrealism, absurdism and epic theatre. Discussions focus upon those landmark productions of modern times in order to be as specific as possible. In one way, it may seem unfortunate that these essays appear separately, artificially dividing the total theatrical scene; yet, in tracing the several competing structures of signals and responses between stage and audience, it is remarkable what continuities are revealed. At all events, my hope is to provide another aid towards a properly stage-centred dramatic criticism, using performance equally with theory as the basis for a history of the stage.

I am grateful to a Fellowship from the National Endowment

for the Humanities of the United States, as well as to Northwestern University, for giving me the opportunity to write this study. I also owe a great debt to the British Library, the Colindale Newspaper Library, the Victoria and Albert Museum and the British Theatre Centre, as well as to the Ford Curtis Theatre Collection of the Hillman Library of the University of Pittsburgh and to the Library of Northwestern University. Robert Schneiderman of Northwestern University, Leonard Powlick of Wilkes-Barre University and John and Barbara Cavanagh of Mottisfont Abbey have been of material assistance to me. The staff of Cambridge University Press have been of great help from beginning to end. A larger kind of debt is owed to the scholarship of countless fine students of the modern drama, and to the creative work of an even greater number of theatre artists.

J. L. S.

1   *The naturalistic revolt*

'Realistic' is a slippery term in dramatic criticism. In 1909, after the best of the realistic plays had been written, Edward Gordon Craig observed in *On the Art of the Theatre* that the artificiality of the Kembles had been supplanted by the more natural Edmund Kean, who had been surpassed in being natural by Macready, who seemed stilted when Henry Irving arrived. In time Antoine made Irving look artificial, and in turn Antoine's acting 'became mere artifice by the side of the acting of Stanislavsky'. What then, asked Craig, did it mean to be 'natural'? He answered, 'I find them one and all to be mere examples of a new artificiality — the artificiality of naturalism' (p. 290). As it is with acting, so it is with playwriting: the old gives way to the new, which in turn grows old. It is axiomatic that each generation feels that its theatre is in some way more 'real' than the last — Euripides over Sophocles, Molière over the *commedia dell'arte*, Goldsmith over Steele, Ibsen over Schiller, Brecht over Ibsen. The claims seem to echo one another. It is, of course, the conception of dramatic reality which changes, and realism must finally be evaluated, not by the style of a play or a performance, but by the image of truth its audience perceives.

The age of Ibsen, Strindberg, Chekhov and the early Shaw thought of itself as realistic in the style as well as the content of its plays, but from our distance it is possible to see that what their actors achieved on the stage was in itself merely another convention. However, if the realistic movement was short-lived (its brief span of thirty years fell between Ibsen's first socially realistic play, *The Pillars of Society*, in 1877 and perhaps Shaw's *The Doctor's Dilemma* in 1906), its impact was powerful. Arthur Miller acknowledged his debt to Ibsen, and Tennessee Williams to Chekhov, fifty years later, even though the mode of their plays had been considerably altered by other pressures.

Yet it may be possible to isolate a characteristic realism, that which, amid a particular controversy, held the late nineteenth-century stage, and to claim that this was the ostensible beginning of the modern drama. This beginning coincided with the scientific revolution which undermined the intellectual optimism of the early years of the century. August Comte's early scientific view of society (*Système de philosophie positive*, 1824), Charles Darwin's biological theory of natural selection (*The Origin of Species*, 1859), the work of the literary historian Hippolyte Taine (*Histoire de la littérature anglaise*, 1864) and the physiologist Claude Bernard (*Introduction a l'étude de la médecine experimentale*, 1865) and Karl Marx's idea of economic man (*Das Kapital*, 1867) together reflect this revolution. The parallel literary movement in France, represented by such naturalistic novelists as Balzac, Flaubert and Zola, accordingly encouraged the emergence of a different kind of play and a different kind of performance to match it.

The new play and its mode of production were in conscious rebellion against the characteristically romantic form of drama popular at the time. The nineteenth century had begun in the full flush of the romantic movement, which affected virtually every form of artistic expression by its mood of radical idealism, spontaneity of feeling and faith in the visionary imagination. In the theatre, the movement was particularly associated with political dissent and unrest after the French Revolution, and it exulted in a new-found freedom of spirit and boldly challenged established values. In Germany especially, Lessing's *Hamburgische Dramaturgie* had rejected the formality of the French classical model for tragedy, and the drama of *Sturm und Drang* (storm and stress) in the theatre of Goethe and Schiller swept the stage with plays of passionate nationalism which glorified figures of heroic proportions. The movement spread rapidly across Europe, and in the process of popularization became as mechanical as the classical tragedy it supplanted.

The romantic ideal for drama was enshrined in a famous manifesto of 1827, the Preface to *Cromwell* of Victor Hugo (1802–85). In elaborate terms, Hugo scorned the neoclassical laws of dramatic unity: the only laws should be those of 'nature'. Taking Shakespeare as its model, the stage should claim its natural freedom of time and place, and allow the sublime and the grotesque, tragedy and comedy, to meet and mingle as in life. In 1830 these new principles were applied by Hugo at the Théâtre Française in his romantic historical melodrama in verse, *Hernani*. This event has been claimed as the most important in nineteenth-century dramatic history. The production caused a riot, the champions of the old ways confronting in the theatre itself those of the new – this was the first of the many public rows which punctuate the story of the modern stage. Victor Hugo won his battle, and although his play was very far from representing real life on the stage, the way had been opened for the coming of modern realism.

At its most vulgar level, the romantic theatre produced a sensational drama of strong emotions and unequivocal moral sentiment. In Britain and America, domestic drama, or 'the melodrama', discovered a simple formula for success which continues to work well in the popular media even today. The leading characters of melodrama, persecuted by villainy and evil in the shape of obvious social injustice, wealth or power, might be expected to bear every torment, feel every moral temptation, sufficient to lend their audience the vicarious excitement of suffering with them. Yet the spectator could share every trembling emotion in the comforting knowledge that providence would eventually intervene and virtue would always triumph. Thus vice and virtue were at bottom a practical business, one in which the virtuous would be rewarded in proportion to their suffering. It was a neat conception for popular consumer art, and it developed the typical stock company of actors who repeated their stereotypes of moral black and white from play to play. The style of acting followed the given formula, with bold, confident gestures reinforced by an appropriately rhetorical speech strong with *sententiae*, and everything else on the stage down to the costume and make-up conveyed clear indications of the social and moral condition of the characters. As the mechanics of the theatre developed behind the proscenium arch, scenery became increasingly spectacular, but it too was required to signal a necessary quality of vice or virtue, peril or security, by the atmosphere of the set. This drama was essentially romantic, joyfully unreal, a concoction of trite situations and petty tricks which worked wonderfully well within the formula.

Led by Eugène Scribe and his immediate successor Victorien Sardou, both men of immense theatrical skill, the romantic drama in Paris drew upon the popular formula, embellished it with over-emphatic speech, gave it a contemporary appeal with a touch of revolutionary sentiment, and specifically arranged the story to capture and hold the interest of a general audience. In translation, the plays of Scribe and Sardou also found enthusiastic audiences everywhere in Europe and America, and provided models for every second-rate playwright. The best plays of Edward Bulwer-Lytton, Tom Taylor and T. W. Robertson in London owed their success to the Scribean pattern, and later playwrights who rebelled against the romantic drama, even Ibsen, Oscar Wilde and Bernard Shaw, nevertheless made use of the very devices they were attacking. Under Scribe's hand, the French style of play acquired the apt name of *la pièce bien faite*, 'the well-made play', and the term eventually became synonymous with any mechanical playwriting which placed too much emphasis upon an efficient plot and a satisfied box-office. Scribe's own total of 374 works for the theatre imply a particular efficiency in managing himself, his collaborators and his audience, as well as the ingredients of a play. The well-made plays of Émile Augier and Dumas *fils* added a new dimension to this drama by using the formula to make a moral point. This was the beginning of the play of ideas, or *la pièce à thèse*. In the kind of social problem play Dumas wrote, an increasing show of interest in the social background of the characters could lend a moral point the force of realism, but every time mechanical plotting confounded a brave intention: the evidence always seemed to be rigged.

The formula for the well-made play was iron-clad. Coincidences in the form of misplaced documents, mistaken identities, lost letters, might be frequent, but the succession of events in a Scribean melodrama was up to a point logical and plausible. The focus of the stage was always on a leading character, the *hero* or *heroine* or both, with whom the audience was expected to *empathize* (I italicize the technical terms here). In the *exposition* of the hero's situation, the audience was told all it needed to know about what had happened in the past, before the curtain rose, as it were. With this information in mind, it could understand and accept the subsequent *complication* of the action, usually caused by the hero's rival, the villain, or some form of obstruction. Matters would grow worse, and tension would be built up as the hero's fortunes seemed destined for disaster. This *reversal* (roughly equivalent to the *peripeteia* of Greek tragedy) was designed specifically to create suspense, and would delay the *resolution* or *dénouement* of the play. However, the story usually turned upon some secret, of which the audience was aware, but of which the hero knew nothing until the truth was conveniently revealed at the critical moment (not unlike the Greek *anagnorisis* or *recognition*). In the judgment of the critic Francisque Sarcey, this was the *scène à faire*, or *obligatory scene*, and at this point the enemy would admit defeat and the hero could celebrate his triumph. The final curtain would then fall without much delay.

Although the well-made play might introduce some political satire, social criticism or even subtlety of character, any of this was subordinate to the contrivances of the plotting; indeed, in his preface to *La Haine* Sardou confessed that he invented the *scène à faire* first, and then worked out his plot backwards. It is little wonder that characters and situations looked much the same from play to play. Yet it was an immensely successful arrangement, and well into the twentieth century the aspiring playwright could still have found rules for writing a well-made play as laid down by William Archer in his *Play-Making: A Manual of Craftsmanship* (1912) or, in America, by George Pierce Baker, director of the famous workshop at Harvard, in his *Dramatic Technique* (1919).

The realistic rebellion, when it came, seemed to many people unpleasant, consciously shocking. In general, the realist of this time was in rebellion against romantic situations and characterization, and tried to put on the stage only what he could verify by observing ordinary life. In the nineteenth century this usually meant middle-class life, and even then the whole truth about ordinary life might suffer from distortion when he tried to surprise his audience into seeing what he wished it to. Like Ibsen, he tried to write dialogue which avoided poetic flights and excessive sentiment, but which corresponded to 'the genuine, plain language spoken in real life' (Ibsen's letter to Lucie Wolf, 25 May 1883), although the demands of a highly defined stage action and the rigid structure of a theatrical plot usually inhibited any accurate reproduction of actual speech.

Much stronger demands might force the realist to depart even farther from verisimilitude, and be even more selective in the material that made up his play. 'Naturalistic' is a critical term which is also slippery, but which may be applied rather more specifically to those playwrights of the so-called 'naturalistic movement', writers who were committed to presenting a specially angled view of real life, as we shall see. The scientific naturalist tried to show that powerful forces governed human lives, forces of which we might not be fully aware and over which we might have little control – the forces of heredity and environment. His play bore witness to the instinctive behaviour of men and women, and his characters and their situations had to seem representative of their class or age group, sex or economic group, with the consequent loss of that essential individuality we know to be also characteristic of life. The paradox grows greater when, in trying to teach their audience a social lesson, some writers lost the scientific objectivity which constituted their reason for writing a realistic play in the first place. Those who showed dramatic bias were legion.

2 Early theory: Zola

Thérèse Raquin (1873)

It was the novelist Émile Zola (1840–1902) who first outlined a theory of naturalism in literature. He regarded his novels, some of which he later turned into plays, as clinical laboratories in which he might scientifically explore the consequences upon his characters of their birth and background. Inevitably his creatures appeared to be the victims of society, and all his conclusions seemed pessimistic.

Zola took the opportunity to write challenging theoretical prefaces to his plays, and the preface to *Thérèse Raquin* is among the most famous of them. He also collected and expanded the dramatic criticism he wrote for the press in Paris under the titles *Le Naturalisme au théâtre* and *Nos auteurs dramatiques*; these books appeared as two of the six volumes of criticism he published in 1880 and 1881. A chapter on the theatre is also included in *Le Roman expérimental*, which was one of the six, and drew heavily upon the notion of scientific method as propounded by Claude Bernard. Although Zola's plays and the dramatic versions of his novels do not live up to his precepts, these critical writings had the effect of making him the champion of the naturalistic movement in his time.

Thérèse Raquin (1867) was widely regarded as the first milestone of the movement. It was a grim tale of sexual passion in a lower middle-class setting. It told of Thérèse's adulterous love, the murder by drowning of her sickly husband, and her subsequent guilt and final suicide in a pact with her lover, Laurent. In 1873 Zola turned the novel into a play in order to help the cause of naturalism in the theatre and to bring drama into line with parallel developments in fiction. The play was produced by Hippolyte Hostein and it was moderately successful (the 1879 adaptation of *L'Assommoir*, which ran for 300 performances, was his best success). *Thérèse Raquin* certainly exemplified Zola's recurrent theme, the pressure of character and the past on events, but it was hardly the realistic slice of life he aimed at. Its characteristic style has Thérèse muttering, for example, 'Assassin, assassin!', with the stage direction, 'Elle est prise de spasmes, chancelle jusqu'au lit, veut se retenir à un des rideaux qu'elle arrache, et reste un instant adossée un mur, haletante et terrible' (III. vi). ('Murderer, murderer!'. . . 'She is seized with spasms, staggers over to the bed and catches hold of the bed curtains, dragging them down. She leans for a moment against the wall breathing hard, a terrifying sight.')

However atmospheric the darkness of the set, however detailed the behaviour and activity of the characters, however closely observed their inner struggles, however inevitable the play's end, its mechanics conformed all too obtrusively with the pattern of the well-made play. Its elements of overstressed sensationalism and impending human disaster implicitly denied the naturalistic requirement of being dispassionate and scientific. Although it was only Zola's emphatic way of urging his cause, the characteristic tone of the play was all towards the sordid and the squalid. Zola's scientific claims no doubt permitted him to select an ugly subject, just as 'a doctor cannot be criticized for studying a revolting venereal disease', as René Wellek puts it in *A History of Modern Criticism* (vol. IV, p. 16), but in his novels and plays, as well as in his criticism, Zola conveyed the distinct impression that he liked to shock. None of this is as important as the thinking that prompted the play, however, and when it appeared *Thérèse Raquin* provoked violent discussion.

Zola's stated philosophy, both of the novel and the drama, was one of absolute objectivity, with setting, characterization and dialogue rendered so close to actual life that an audience would be convinced by the illusion of its reality. A playwright had only to reproduce man's environment, endow it with human life and show that one produced the other, and what had seemed small and insignificant could be important and urgent.

He was right in believing that the driving force behind the thought and literature of the age was that of naturalism, and although he was not in a position to identify its sources, he recognized the significance of the rise of the natural sciences in the previous century and that the nineteenth century was the age of the experimental method. He believed that naturalism had appeared in the novel first because the theatre was hidebound by conventions which were slow to change; he could not see, as Strindberg was to see later, that a smaller and less popular audience would permit a more rapid change. Zola's target was the established French theatre of the romantic drama and the boulevard melodrama, the theatre of Augier and Dumas *fils* with their complaisant claims to being realistic. He particularly distrusted the vogue for historical drama because of its open invitation to spectacle and swagger; even today we know what he means from our contemporary examples of big costume films and pretentious period plays. Zola compared this colourful nonsense with the serious French novel of Stendhal, Balzac, Flaubert and the brothers Goncourt, and what they had achieved in fine character detail and analysis.

The best novelists had rejected romantic characters, mere symbolic fictions representing virtue or vice, and had refused to invent grand romantic scenes in which any true observation of human conduct had to bow before the demands of sentiment. They had abandoned the sort of outworn plotting which seemed to Zola like 'a childish game of tying threads in order to enjoy untying them again'. With their new objectivity had disappeared any need for majestic speech and noble sentiments. Now it was time for the theatre not only to strip the stage of its artificial trappings, but also of its false content. But even Zola did not reckon with the inflexibility of the profession: the style of acting is inseparable from the way a play works, and he could not change the actors overnight. Indeed, the great realists, Ibsen, Shaw, Chekhov and the rest, each in his own way, had to accommodate or do battle with the very actors upon whom they depended.

Zola recognized that the dramatist lacked the freedom of the novelist, and further encouraged the break with the restrictions of the neoclassical unities. The novelist could be prodigal with time and space, and had to woo only the solitary reader sitting by his fireside rather than a spectator sitting in a crowd. However, Zola would not admit the inferiority of the theatre as a vehicle, although he predicted its quick death if it did not bend with the times. He argued that in the history of the theatre, the drama had always managed to adapt itself, and would do so again, bringing its special strengths of immediacy and intensity to the naturalistic movement.

In all his dramatic criticism, Zola emphasized the importance of characterization as the best measure of a play's truthfulness. The characters of the romantic drama were too facile, too standardized. He pointed to the attention given to character in the French classical drama of Corneille, Racine and Molière, and found the heroes of their nineteenth-century successors to be wooden puppets, mere abstractions of duty, patriotism, superstition or maternal love. The new naturalistic drama would return to the analysis of character, except that now the characters would be ordinary people in their natural setting, and the play would examine the physical and social influences that made them what they were.

Stage scenery might be nothing but canvas and paint, but it was the theatre's equivalent of the element of description in the novel. Moreover, scenery on the stage remained vividly before the eyes for as long as the curtain was up, a background and environment for the characters which would be faithful to the author's conception. A factory, a mine, a market, a railway station or a racetrack could supply all the colour and life any play could desire, even when the aim was not one of decoration, but of dramatic utility. In his thinking about realism, Zola believed that it was necessary for every play to have its appropriate setting; he could not conceive that an abstract or neutral background might heighten the detail and particularity of dialogue and behaviour. For him the rule was that a lifelike setting encouraged lifelike costumes, which encouraged lifelike dialogue.

Zola was more acute in his analysis of the romantic theatre when he recognized that the language of the play was the key to change. Nineteenth-century stage speech, itself a product of neo-classical tragedy, was associated with a special 'theatre voice' and a rich declamatory manner, although all the full-blooded passions, the romantic sentiment and bravado, the excess of cliché and platitude, were actually a direct result of thin-blooded, stock characters. If the moment was serious, the language was sonorous, balanced, rhetorical; if lighter in vein, it was perforce witty, paradoxical, scintillating. None of it had to do with the way people really spoke. Zola further recognized that, in spite of the range of characters in the plays of Dumas *fils*, for example, they all spoke the same stage language. Therefore, the new dialogue should be flexible and precise, and convey the tone and feeling of a character's individuality. This important suggestion would be followed up later, particularly by Ibsen.

All these principles supported Zola's essential requirement that the theatre should not *lie*; he claimed that he was 'the honest soldier of truth'. We may smile now at the notion that literature could ever become a science, because a fiction can never prove anything; but the 'experimental' approach of naturalism could strongly inform the creative imagination and provide a vital new impulse for art, as indeed it did. Zola believed that art and literature should serve the inquiring mind, investigating, analysing and reporting on man and society, seeking the facts and the logic behind human life. Nor need the new drama be deficient in 'poetry', for truth would encourage the poetry of humanity: reality had greatness in itself. So Zola awaited the arrival of a genius, a true innovator who would change a stage soaked with 'the grey rain of stale mediocrity', and speed the rebirth of the theatre.

This innovator was to be Ibsen, who, as it happened, greatly disliked being compared with Zola: 'Zola', he said, 'descends into the sewer to bathe in it; I to cleanse it.' However that may be, the real question remained whether Zola or Ibsen or anyone else could change the style of declamatory acting which had made the romantic theatre so popular. What if the actress playing the new Thérèse behaved just like the old Camille? Unless the profession changed, the impact of a bold new naturalistic theatre would not be felt.

3   *A new production style: the Saxe-Meiningen Company*

Luckily, certain developments in theatre practice at this time began to catch the attention of Europe. When Duke Georg II (1826—1914) ascended the ducal throne of the tiny Thuringian Duchy of Saxe-Meiningen in 1866, his interest as an amateur in history and archaeology, art, design and the theatre, and in particular his enthusiasm for the realistic authenticity of Charles Kean's Shakespeare productions at the Princess's Theatre in London, prompted him to take an unusually personal interest in the work of the Meiningen theatre. The Duke was a reformer who had been repelled by the artificial conventions of mid-nineteenth-century staging and acting, and he argued for having one man, the artistic director, in total control of a production, a practice which had in fact been growing in the German theatre since the eighteenth century.

Elsewhere at this time the scene designer was a law unto himself, and as for the star actor, who was frequently the all-powerful actor-manager also, he could decide upon his interpretation of a role without reference to the rest of the cast, or without even taking a rehearsal. From the Meiningen productions we can recognize the beginning of the modern idea of the *régisseur*, a director responsible for the total conception, the overall style and every detail of a production. There was no actor-manager in the Meiningen company, and the star system did not exist: instead, the company worked together as an ensemble in which the leading actor from one play might be expected to play a member of the crowd in another, so that the work of everyone in the company was regarded as important to the whole artistic effort. The Duke was the master-mind himself, with the assistance of Ludwig Chronegk, a fierce disciplinarian, as his stage manager. Josef Levinsky, the great Viennese actor, believed the Duke to be the best director that Germany had known.

When the new principles were put into practice, the planning stage of a production became of primary importance, and the period necessary for rehearsal often lasted for months. The time was used to work out in meticulous detail, on paper and on the stage, the blocking or grouping of the characters and their moves. Where in the past crowd scenes had been left to look after themselves, now they were planned as if a group of actors were a single character, but with every supernumerary treated as an individual. The result was an astonishing realism in performance.

Fortunately, the Duke wrote an article for the *Deutsche Bühne* in which he recorded some of his principles of directing a play. All of it will seem obvious to us today, since each item has now become common practice.

On the stage picture. He tried to avoid symmetrical grouping and centrally placed figures because they were lifeless and boring, and he quoted Boileau in his support: 'L'ennui naquit un jour de l'uniformité.' For the same reason, parallels and straight lines were bad. In order to suggest continuous action, the stage should always convey a sense of motion; thus an actor standing on a stairway should rest one foot above the other. He warned against the in-congruity of having an actor move against a set designed in perspec-tive, lest he appear disproportionately too big or too small. Nor should he touch a canvas flat lest it shake. Real props should not be set against painted objects, nor should live actors be expected to compete with painted scenery; however, an actor who touched a piece of real furniture would thereby suggest its material reality.

On acting in period plays. Rehearsals should be taken in costume, so that the actor could grow accustomed to wearing unfamiliar clothes.

On the treatment of crowd scenes. Hired supers should be trained in small groups, each led by a more experienced actor. Crowd noise should not be made or spoken in unison, but be transformed into particular words and then learned and acted like any other part. Any regularity in a line of heads, or any similarity of posture, was to be avoided by having some actors kneeling or bending. A super might never look at the audience. A crowd might be used partly to cover the removal of the dead or wounded. In order to suggest a 'vast' crowd, supers should seem to disappear into the wings, as if there were unseen numbers offstage.

In this way every detail was carefully arranged to promote the all-important illusion of real life, and it is not hard to see that the new naturalistic drama would find these methods highly appropriate to its intentions. Stage detail of this order matched the detail of the new realistic characters, and would help them to be seen against a closely observed background. Georg actually visited Fotheringay and Domrémy before designing the sets for Bjørnson's *Mary Stuart in Scotland* and Schiller's *The Maid of Orleans*, and Ibsen even sent him a detailed account of a middle-class Norwegian house in preparation for the Meiningen production of *Ghosts*. This concern for historical authenticity in costume and décor today seems pedantic and mistaken in its pictorial treatment of Shakespeare and Schiller, whose poetic drama sought to escape the limitations of realism, but it was absolutely right for the conviction of actuality necessary for the successful production of much of Ibsen and his successors. In *Ibsen's Dramatic Technique*, p. 54, P.F.D. Tennant goes so far as to suggest that Ibsen's very full stage directions were justified by the Meiningen method of stage production, and it is no surprise that the work of the company became an admired standard for the tribe of new directors who led the independent theatre movement at the end of the century.

The company took Berlin by storm in 1874, and travelled Europe demonstrating their revolutionary approach. In 1876, Ibsen saw them perform his early play, *The Pretenders*, in Berlin. In 1881, William Archer saw their *Julius Caesar*, among other plays, in London. In 1888, André Antoine saw their production of *William Tell* in Brussels. Stanislavsky first saw them in St Petersburg, and subsequently spent a year with them. Even Henry Irving's crowd work improved after he saw them in London. Antoine and Stanislavsky both claimed that it was the Meiningen company which inspired their new approach to the theatre, and detailed rehearsal, disciplined ensemble playing and the unity and consistency of a production became the hallmarks of the Théâtre-Libre and the Moscow Art Theatre.

When the company came to London and presented a repertory of Schiller's first and last 'revolutionary' dramas, *Die Räuber* (*The Robbers*) and *William Tell*, together with Shakespeare's *Julius Caesar*, *Twelfth Night* and *The Winter's Tale*, there were few critics who did not take special note of the crowd scenes and praise them lavishly. For a rare example of a reviewer who withheld his enthusiasm, the

1. Shakespeare, *Julius Caesar*, 1879. Sketch by the Duke of Saxe-Meiningen based upon drawings from the Archaeological Institute, Rome. Act III, the forum scene.

correspondent of *The Athenaeum* of 4 June 1881 declared that the principal gain was only in the manner in which those who were little or nothing more than supers wore the costumes of a bygone age, and took 'an intelligent part in actions and movements of which they can have had no experience in real life'. He otherwise found the Forum scene of *Julius Caesar* incongruous: 'The violence of the outbreak seemed, however, out of keeping with the quasi-symmetrical arrangement of the tableaux' — a comment which must have puzzled and annoyed the Duke. In Schiller's play, happily, this omniscient critic found the arrangement of the robbers' camp on the banks of the Danube more natural and to his taste, although he could not forbear a critical comment on the men's costumes, which he found 'too varied'. Suddenly the standards of realism in the theatre had become very fine.

Reviewing the same production of *Julius Caesar* for *The London Figaro* of 4 June 1881, William Archer reported that the crowd did not merely provide a background for the Tribunes: 'On the contrary, Flavius and Marullus mix with it and elbow with it, sometimes almost hidden in its midst. It has all the uncertain fluctuations of an actual crowd. Its splendid drill produces the effect of absolute freedom from drill.' When Antony delivered his speech in the Forum, 'He did not address himself to the imagination of the audience, but to the living and moving populace before him. . . It is rather by inference than by personal sensation or intuition that we recognize the power of Mark Antony's oratory. We see how it moves the crowd, and by an act of judgment we decide that it should and must be so moved.' This remark might be pondered by all those directors who would have Antony in this scene seem to address the real audience as if they were citizens of Rome like the on-stage audience.

The aim was to create the illusion of natural space within the unnaturally rigid frame of the proscenium arch. In the production of *William Tell*, Archer was delighted with the way in which every leaf was painted a different colour, and with the method by which an effect of rain was achieved by lights playing on a moving backcloth. He admired the use of steam to suggest the dust rising when the Swiss tore down an Austrian castle, and noted with approval how small boys wearing beards were made to stand on scaffolding at the back of the stage to encourage the effect of distance. He failed to note, however, that he was not intended to note the device in the first place. When Antoine saw this production seven years later, he wrote an enthusiastic letter to Sarcey, and this letter, reprinted in S. M. Waxman's book, *Antoine and the Théâtre Libre*, is a prime document in this history:

> They showed us things absolutely new and very instructive. Their crowds are not like ours, composed of elements picked haphazardly, working men hired for dress rehearsals, badly clothed, and unaccustomed to wearing strange and uncomfortable costumes, especially when they are exact. Immobility is almost always required of the crowds on our stage, whereas the supernumeraries of the Meiningen crowds must act and mime their characters. Don't understand by that that they force the note and that the attention is distracted from the protagonists. No, the tableau is complete, and in whatever direction you may look, you fix your eyes on a detail in the situation or character. At certain moments, the power is incomparable. (pp. 95–6)

2. Interior of the Moscow Art Theatre about 1910. See also ch. 10, pp. 70–81.

Antoine was also impressed by the way a character on the stage could apparently control the noise and movement of the crowd with a gesture, and remarked how the supers did not look at the audience but at the actor addressing them. He complained, however, about the erection and painting of the scenery, and was particularly disturbed by what seemed to be squeaking floorboards high up in the mountains. For his taste, the torrential rain stopped too abruptly, and the mountaineers displayed hands and knees that were too white — 'clean as if they were at the Opéra Comique'.

It is interesting to note that Antoine also observed another Meiningen phenomenon, a small matter perhaps, but one which he was not to forget. The murder of Gessler included a superb touch:

> Gessler's way was blocked by a beggar and his two children who played a long scene of supplication with their backs to the audience, while Tell looked on. Seeing this, you would have agreed that fitting use of full-back positions contributed greatly to the actor's conviction and the spectator's illusion.

Porel had tried such acting at the Odéon in the 1880s, but a proscenium actor rarely dared to play with his back to the audience, whether it was realistic or not. Now unending possibilities of deceiving the audience seemed to offer themselves to the actors, directors and writers who watched this formidable company from Germany, and any effect which might contribute to the sacred ideal of realistic illusion was greedily absorbed.

4 *Ibsen's contribution to realism*

A Doll's House (1879), *Ghosts* (1881)

At the time when Henrik Ibsen (1823–1906) saw the Meiningen company perform his play *The Pretenders* in Berlin in 1876, it ran for nine nights to 'wild applause'; and ten years later Georg II was among the first to produce the controversial *Ghosts*. Theirs was a mutual admiration which was to make a true contribution to the realistic movement.

Ibsen had begun writing plays when he was twenty, and had had his first play produced at the Christiana (Oslo) Theatre two years later. Of greater importance in our context, however, is the fact that for six years he was stage manager and director at the National Theatre in Bergen, where he directed no fewer than 145 productions, more than half of them by Scribe or in the Scribean manner. Then he spent another five years as artistic director of the Norwegian Theatre in Christiana. He had therefore had a strong apprenticeship in the old kind of professional theatre from 1851 to 1862, producing and writing within the romantic tradition long before he began his revolutionary departure into realism with *The Pillars of Society* in 1877. To this point must be added another. The well-known speech Ibsen made to the university students who had honoured him with a torchlight procession on 10 September 1874 was made well before his name had became synonymous with the notorious stage of *A Doll's House* and *Ghosts*, but it marked an important step in Ibsen's self-awareness as a playwright, and drew attention to an essential ingredient in the great plays which were to come. That speech insisted that the artist must possess some experience of the life he was trying to create. In some degree everything that Ibsen wrote during the turbulent years of his realistic revolt was for him also a felt experience.

After *Brand* and *Peer Gynt* his plays increasingly reject the old methods. Technically, he found the *scène à faire* too useful to throw out: he needed it to project as powerfully as possible what it meant for a Nora or a Mrs Alving to discover the truth about their marriages. But signs of a new set of values, personal and urgent, showed themselves when he broke with the mechanics of the Scribean formula. His characters revealed the importance of the past more sincerely, and their memories and relationships one with another were more deeply thought out. Above all, his themes were his own. As he said in a letter to his publisher, Frederick Hegel, on 31 October 1868, he had begun consciously to dramatize the 'forces and frictions of modern life', a process which was to result in the more realistic, but still lightweight, social comedy, *The League of Youth* (1869). This was his first play to be written in modern, colloquial prose, but its conventions were still those of a dying drama. Of *Emperor and Galilean* (1873), he claimed to have seen everything happen, as it were, 'before his own eyes', and in letters to Edmund Gosse on 20 February 1873 and 15 January 1874, he said he had written the play in prose in order to convince his reader that the events had actually happened. For all this, however, the complicated metaphysical theme of this sprawling epic of Roman history appears to be a step backwards into private drama.

Ibsen had witnessed the Saxe-Meiningen company at work by this time, but his particular association with the young Danish critic Georg Brandes marked the turning point. Brandes's lectures and articles called for writers to turn against romantic idealism, and urged that Scandinavian literature grapple with contemporary social problems. He had been puzzled by the determinism of *Emperor and Galilean*, but pleased with its psychological insight, which he considered its strength. It seems likely that Brandes, who had looked at the latest French drama and found in it a recurring theme, the link between morality and money, and even a hint of what was to become the Ibsenite 'new woman' with a mind of her own, was in part responsible for prompting Ibsen's pursuit of realism in *The Pillars of Society*. For this play Ibsen appeared to borrow from *The League of Youth* its prose realism and its examination of provincial life as a microcosm of the world beyond, and then to graft on to these some of the character psychology found in *Emperor and Galilean*.

At any rate, Brandes's demand for contemporary social problems on the stage begins to be answered in Ibsen. The Norwegian background is increasingly present, with a sense of the harsh terrain of mountains and fjords shutting off one community from another, and each small town managing its own problems, giving local politics and social mores an unusual prominence. The stern Calvinism which contributed to the national character made the moral issues of the mid-nineteenth century particularly fierce. The time had come for the stage to be peopled with creatures with genuine roots and authentic backgrounds. Causes and effects in society awaited an honest treatment, and vast new territories of theme and content lay open to the scientific explorer. Ibsen's modest beginning, *The Pillars of Society*, is the moral story of Consul Bernick, a small-town ship-builder who has built his marriage and his social position on a lie, and his business on underhand practice. In the last act Bernick confesses his guilt in public, and the play ends 'happily' in the hope that old hypocrisies will give place to the spirit of truth and freedom. Today, this play causes scarcely a ripple. Not only is the confessional ending too facile, but, in spite of signs of a sharper characterization and a more idiosyncratic speech, the noble lines and grand gestures of the play demand the old declamatory acting. James Walter McFarlane, translator of the Oxford *Ibsen*, has remarked how verbose and prolix is the last act: 'the speech-rhythms are — for the dramatic crisis of a modern realistic play — quite astonishingly slow-moving' (vol. v, p. 12). In comparison with *A Doll's House* or *Ghosts, The Pillars of Society* threw out little challenge to its audiences: everyone could comfortably choose the side of righteousness, and both in form and content its satire was somewhat toothless.

By contrast, *A Doll's House* (1879) is almost as topical today as it was a century ago, as recent revivals have shown. Yet even today's critics, like those of the nineteenth century, fail to remark the play's extraordinary technical achievement, because its explosive subject matter is still so obsessive that no room seems left for objective appraisal — a point well made by Michael Meyer in his indispensable biography of Ibsen. If we are overwhelmed by the theme of women's rights and the concept of a woman's duty to herself rather than her self-sacrifice in marriage, perhaps we should be as impressed by the fact that Ibsen had also visualized his Nora right down to the 'blue woollen dress' she wore. He championed the character quite as much as the cause. Of course one must ask why it was that no one could be untouched by the play: but was it only the issue of female emancipation and the relentless slamming of the door with which Nora walked out of Torvald Helmer's life, the whole sensational package, which made this play a masterpiece? Few of these effects would have been felt so strongly had not the quieter strategies of Ibsen's work prepared for them: in the several revisions of the play Nora's character grew more and more subtle in an increasingly rich subtext.

In her 1928 lecture to the Royal Society of Arts, *Ibsen and the Actress*, the American actress Elizabeth Robins argued that in his script Ibsen actually 'collaborated' with his actor. She cited the moment when in *The Master Builder* Hilda sat on a little stool at Aline's feet and hugged her knees on the line, 'Ah, here one can sit and sun oneself like a cat', and she observed how the warmth and sensuousness of those words were set in contrast with her chilling statement a moment later, 'I have just come up out of a tomb'. When Robins played Hedda Gabler later, she remarked Ibsen's 'supreme faculty of giving his actors the clue — the master-key', for she had felt Hedda 'warm to my touch' and, in spite of Hedda's repellent qualities, saw her as 'pitiable in her hungry loneliness'. 'Make no mistake', she concluded, 'you must let Ibsen play you, rather than insist on your playing Ibsen' (p. 56).

Although the perceptive George Moore, like other commentators who could not forget the shocking message of *A Doll's House*, found the play 'wooden', 'hard' and 'illogical', no actress playing Nora then or now could fail to be struck by the number of non-verbal details with which Ibsen built up her character: at the opening of the play, Nora's joy in her Christmas tree and the presents she has bought, the toys for the children; her extravagant tipping of the porter; her pleasure in her macaroons and the childlike way she eats them, hiding the bag from Torvald and surreptitiously wiping her mouth; her act of taking the money from him, and then pulling the button on his coat for more. The business of the macaroons and the money was added in the final version, and is a clear indication that Ibsen knew he was creating a particular life, and making sure that his actress could enrich her performance by working with such details. Nora's games with the children are nicely held in reserve as a foil for the sinister entrance of Krogstad; although this was possibly a retreat towards the melodramatic, it was also a device by which the whole situation was embellished in order to dramatize Nora's two lives. The earlier version omitted the second-act Christmas tree; in performance, it stood there stripped of its ornaments, looking bedraggled, its candles burned down, lending a special atmosphere to the stage. In this act Ibsen also added the flesh-coloured stockings with which Nora flirts with Dr Rank, and at the end of this act, when Nora must distract Torvald from finding Krogstad's incriminating letter, Ibsen substituted for the Turkish dance to Anitra's song from *Peer Gynt* the new symbolism of the

tarantella, danced wildly to a tambourine by Nora with her hair
fallen loose. And in the third act, this immodest wife of a sedate
bank manager wears her Neapolitan costume with its large black
shawl in order to continue the exotic image of the tarantella — all
this before she changes, symbolically again, into her drab, everyday
clothes in preparation for her shattering final exit.

Yet even the reader for the Royal Theatre, Copenhagen, which
first staged the play, found Nora's action in walking out psycho-
logically 'unsatisfying', and there were not many like the reviewer
for *Folkets Avis* of 24 December 1879 who noted its unusual economy
of method and its absence of blood, tears and other melodramatics.
There is a minimum of inflated language at the end of *A Doll's House*,
and it ends promptly when its point is made. The play offered a true
advance in style, but it was its content which provoked outrage and
hostility. For the German production, Ibsen was compelled to write
a so-called 'happy ending', lest it was rewritten without consulting
him: the German ending has Nora, torn between her wish to leave
her husband and her urge to stay with her children, merely sink to

3. Ibsen, *A Doll's House*, Royal Court Theatre, Copenhagen,
1879. Act II, the tarantella scene.

the floor. It is as significant that, at a time when Ibsen's name was a household word throughout Europe, the play did not appear on the British stage for ten years, or on the French for fifteen. Indeed, the play's adventures in the English-speaking world imply a total distrust of its theme. America saw a first English production in Milwaukee in 1882, and this was an emasculated version by W. M. Lawrence entitled *The Child Wife*. In 1884, London was treated to Henry Arthur Jones's adaptation of the play into an English setting, entitled *Breaking a Butterfly*; in this, Torvald became Humphrey, Nora became Flora or Flossie, and, needless to say, Humphrey and Flossie were tearfully reconciled at the fall of the curtain. In 1885, London also saw a limping amateur performance in aid of none other than the Society for the Prevention of Cruelty to Children. In one translation by a certain T. Weber, Nora's famous curtain line became, 'That cohabitation between you and me might become a matrimony!', and Granville-Barker was so struck by this that he thought a prize should be given at the Royal Academy of Dramatic Art to the student who could say the line without making an audience laugh.

London had to wait until 1889 for a fully professional production. This was by Charles Charrington at the Novelty Theatre, Kingsway, in William Archer's translation, with Charrington playing an icy Dr Rank and Charrington's wife, Janet Achurch, aged twenty-five, playing Nora, the first great Ibsen part seen in Britain. It was played, in the eyes of Elizabeth Robins and her friend Marion Lea, to 'a sparse, rather dingy audience' in a 'pokey, dingy theatre'. The production caused the expected stir, and apart from one or two enthusiasts like William Archer and George Bernard Shaw (who was yet to deliver his Fabian lectures on Ibsenism in 1890), it was generally condemned as an example of a morbid and perverted new cult concerned with the degradation of women. It was at this time that Clement Scott, writing in *Theatre* on 1 July 1889, was the first to use the word 'Ibsenite' as a term of opprobrium. Again, any technical achievement in the writing or the acting went unnoticed, other than *The Times*'s facile condemnation of the play's 'almost total lack of dramatic action' and *The People*'s decision that the infamous ending was not only immoral, but 'essentially undramatic'. It was as yet too soon for the general audience to change its way of seeing, and if it did not find the play positively obscene, it found it dreary.

We turn to Elizabeth Robins for any comment on the performance. She was impressed by the 'unstagey' effect of the whole play: it was less like a play than 'like a personal meeting'. How refreshing it was to see Achurch break the rule that a leading actress must always enter in new clothes! She struck a note of gaiety and homeliness: 'You saw her biting into one of the forbidden macaroons, white teeth flashing, blue eyes full of roguery.' She was particularly impressed by Nora's 'warm bright confidence splintering against that tombstone of a man' —Dr Rank. Only the tarantella seemed to be a piece of theatricalism, 'Ibsen's one concession to the effect-hunting that he had come to deliver us from'.

The London production went on tour, arriving in America in 1895. New York audiences applauded Achurch's Nora (as they were to applaud the French Nora, Gabrielle Réjane, in the same season). Achurch and Robins were between them to create the new actress to match Ibsen's new woman, culminating in their respective Heddas in the years to come. The conception of the new woman lay not merely in recognizing her intellect and independence; she was also required to perform in a new way. Audiences had only to compare the excessive emotionality and resonant tones of the girl Margrete in Ibsen's *The Pretenders* of 1863 (with lines like 'Respect a wife's grief!' and 'Blessed be your mouth, even though it curses me now!') with Nora and her richly observed detail of speech and behaviour, to see that the two belonged to different worlds.

William Archer was among the first to recognize that Nora's actress needed to be especially talented mentally and physically. In *The Theatrical World* for 1893, he reported that he had seen the Italian Nora of Eleonora Duse at the Lyric Theatre, and approved her 'spontaneous, effervescent, iridescent' gaiety of the first act. But he found her less satisfying than Achurch, and his reasons are some of those by which naturalistic theatre may be judged. Duse had failed to respond to certain loaded words which called for a more subtle reaction from the actress, as when Krogstad told Nora that her father appeared to have signed the note of hand three days after his death, and again when Torvald suggested that Krogstad should admit the guilt she knew was really hers. Archer also found that

Duse failed to perceive the *hidden rhythm* of the second act, which passed from gloom to gaiety and then to dignity; she had instead painted the whole scene in one colour. But he surprisingly approved her decision to cut back the tarantella, which he too thought was 'Ibsen's last concession to the old technique' and 'beneath her dignity', even though he appreciated a comparable contrast between the Capri costume of the last act and Nora's death-like, ashen face as she wore it.

As time passed, comments of a more technical kind were heard. Writing in *The Saturday Review* of 15 May 1897 about a new production of *A Doll's House* at the Globe Theatre, London, Shaw was able to make a comparison with what he had seen eight years earlier. He found Courtenay Thorpe's Torvald 'overwhelming' for being spoken with genuine feeling: 'We no longer study an object lesson in lord-of-creationism, appealing to our sociological interest only', he said. But Shaw also observed that some of Torvald's more fatuous lines were still uttered as 'points', thereby destroying their realism. (A 'point' in the Victorian theatre was a striking moment in performance when the actor revealed an essential element of character or situation by emphasizing a special piece of business or by speaking a line in an arresting voice; Victorian actors acquired their reputations by punctuating their performance with as many points as possible.) In the production at the Globe, Achurch had revived her memorable Nora, but she replaced the wide-eyed naïveté of her former youthfulness with a less girlish sophistication. For the 1890s, these were all fine considerations in performance criticism, and Shaw concluded his notice by remarking, 'The flattering notion, still current in the profession, that anybody can play Ibsen, is hardly bearing the test of experience.' We shall see how Ibsen's demands upon his actors will grow even more in his progress from Nora to Mrs Alving and Hedda.

Ghosts (1881) was a natural sequel to *A Doll's House*: 'After Nora, Mrs Alving had to come', Ibsen wrote in a letter of 24 June 1882. Mrs Alving is the Nora who was persuaded to stay at home, only to find that her son had inherited venereal disease from his father. The subject of the play was again one of duty and freedom, but it also touched upon all the forbidden topics —syphilis, adultery, free love, incest and euthanasia. Ibsen knew that he was defying social convention, but he had not reckoned with the violence of the hostile reaction to his play. Almost everywhere *Ghosts* was rejected as pathologically obscene, and even well-educated people would not have the book in the house. Ibsen found only a few supporters among students, as always, and liberal thinkers like Bjørnson and Georg Brandes. As for a production of the play, no European theatre would touch it, and it had its first production in Chicago in Norwegian. The play had to wait until 1883 for its first European production, although this was in Swedish: the leading actor-manager in Stockholm, August Lindberg, presented it in the Swedish town of Hälsingborg.

In order to prepare himself for playing Oswald, Lindberg actually visited syphilitic patients in a Copenhagen hospital, and in the event, audiences who sat through the play found the experience intensely moving. The Mrs Alving of the veteran actress Hedvig Charlotte Winter-Hjelm was particularly powerful. According to Lindberg, the play began with the audience holding its breath, and with the horror of the last act, the curtain fell to a spell-bound silence; then a storm of applause burst out. In performance, it seems, the inherent strength of the play defeated its moralizing critics. According to William Archer, who chanced to see Winter-Hjelm's performance later in Christiana, she suffered from a little staginess and 'declamatory bitterness' in her speeches to Manders, but she otherwise played sympathetically and maintained a ladylike manner. But Archer was especially impressed by Oswald, remarking upon Lindberg's pale face, blinking eyes and dreamy pace ('the manner of a man to whom the world has become unreal'), and he concluded that the actor had worked upon his part in extraordinary detail.

London first saw *Ghosts* in 1891, in a private performance at The Royalty Theatre packed to the roof, with a good amateur actress, Mrs Theodore Wright, as Mrs Alving — the first licensed performance was not to be until 1914. This 1891 première was arranged by J. T. Grein and offered as the first production of his newly formed Independent Theatre Society: it was this notorious play which had also opened Berlin's Freie Bühne in 1889. The event shook the West End. There is no need to reprint here the list of abusive epithets which were poured upon the play, upon Ibsen and upon his supporters alike, especially by Clement Scott of *The Daily Telegraph*. These were solemnly collected by Archer in the *Pall Mall Gazette* of 8 April 1891 and gleefully reprinted by Shaw in *The Quintessence of Ibsenism* the same year. Only A. B. Walkley, writing in *The Star*, found the play 'a great spiritual drama' and declared it to be a masterpiece. Again a naturalistic theme was all-consuming, so that the play's new method was scarcely remarked.

When the play was revived in New York in 1903, William Winter's comment was damning: 'The Ibsen Drama seldom affords opportunity for acting — a chief reason being that most of the characters in it are so radically false to nature' (*The Wallet of Time*,

4. Ibsen, *Ghosts*, Hälsingborg, 1883. First European production, directed by August Lindberg. Act III, with Lindberg and Hedvig Charlotte Winter-Hjelm.

vol. 2, p. 567). This was a simple refusal to watch, and others had decided differently. Walkley believed that an absence of over-acting was right for Ibsen, and according to C. E. Montague in *Dramatic Values*, Janet Achurch's perfomance as Mrs Alving in 1907 was able to set a new standard of sensitive acting: 'When she stands behind Oswald's chair to hide the despair in her face, and struggles to cheer him with hopeless lies about hope, the beauty and tenderness in Miss Janet Achurch's acting was a thing not to be figured in words, for one art cannot re-do the masterpiece of another.' The Mrs Alving of Eleonora Duse in 1923 was, on the other hand, an 'exquisite creature, moving from grief to grief in some grey saraband of woe'; so James Agate put it in *The Sunday Times*, but she was not Ibsen's 'still rebellious woman whose egotism, hardly baulked, breaks out again in bitter mockery of Pastor Manders'. As early as 2 August 1883, in a letter to Lindberg, Ibsen had insisted on the necessity for 'ruthless honesty' in performance, and he added:

> The dialogue must seem perfectly natural, and the manner of expression must differ from character to character. Many changes in the dialogue can be made during rehearsals, where one can easily hear what sounds natural and un-forced, and also what needs to be revised over and over again until finally it sounds completely real and believable. The effect of the play depends a great deal on making the spectator feel as if he were actually sitting, listening and looking at events happening in real life. (Translated Evert Sprinchorn.)

It will seem strange to us today that this needed to be said. Compared with the romantic drama, Ibsen's social plays in fact have little physical action; the emphasis is all on a new psychological contest of minds as the characters circle and evade the taboo subjects.

The forbidden subject-matter of *Ghosts*, and the continual hints at the Victorian 'double standard' of sexual conduct, were as much responsible for the notable indirectness of the play's new dialogue as its excessive use of the Sophoclean method of telling the story in retrospect, that is, as if the main events had already taken place before the curtain rose. So much of what is said is a cover for what is deeply felt, as well as for what is supposed to have been previously experienced. In his biography Michael Meyer explains, 'Mrs Alving and Manders especially spend much of the time circling round a subject to which they dread referring directly, and at these moments the dialogue is oblique, sometimes even opaque' (p. 490). Here, then, was another step towards the new acting. If the playwright is dealing in the unspoken, the actor must search beneath the lines for the feelings he must hide before he can hide them, and the whole concept of a play's 'subtext', with all its attendant demands on composition and performance, start from *Ghosts*. Compared with *A Doll's House*, there are far fewer visual details introduced into the final text, far fewer physical signs of submerged meaning, but the verbal subtleties are outstanding.

In an earlier note for the play, moreover, Ibsen had written, 'Everything is ghosts.' Certainly, an audience reading the title of the play and anticipating its action, will find there ghosts of all kinds from the past, and it will begin to spot them from the rise of the curtain, and not just when Mrs Alving herself hears ominous echoes from the next room in the words of Oswald and Regina. Hidden relationships, the inhibitions of social convention, and secret fears and anxieties lurk everywhere in the play. The forbidden books lie on the table centre-stage like an accusation during the whole action, and, since we never know their content, the audience supplies it and does its worst. The conservatory, shadowy from the endless rain, conceals the skeletons from the past in Mrs Alving's memory and ours too. In a whisper of conspiracy, Regina greets Engstrand, the man with the ever-obtrusive limp; this Engstrand persists with his darkly depraved suggestions for Regina's future; Manders starts as he thinks he sees the image of the dead Alving come alive again in Oswald when the young man enters with a pipe in his mouth. So the house is everywhere haunted, and the mystery lingers to the end. When Ibsen was asked whether Mrs Alving finally gave the poison to her son after the terrifying curtain scene, his reply was a simple, 'I don't know.'

Ronald Gray has recently thrown doubts upon the claim that Ibsen was a master of realistic portrait painting. In *Ibsen — A Dissenting View* (1977), Gray accuses the playwright of having sacrificed character to plot, reducing Torvald in *A Doll's House*, for example, to a stereotype of a Victorian husband as a way of justifying the excessive gesture of Nora's decision to leave him. Ibsen is also charged with ignoring consistency of character in Mrs Alving in *Ghosts*, since she is at first shocked by Oswald's flirting with Regina in the next room, only to consent soon afterwards to their incestuous marriage. Even those characters traditionally considered to be Ibsen's richest, like Rebecca West of *Rosmersholm* and the monumental Hedda Gabler, are declared deficient in some respect. It is possible to multiply instances which suggest that Ibsen allowed his plots to determine his characterization, and it is certainly a good thing to examine propositions that are normally taken for granted. Yet these arguments are of the closet, and Ibsen in performance is another matter. Degrees of 'realism', of what seems real, change from age to age, of course, but the quality of enduring realistic detail in a characterization may be tested only in performance over a period of time. The test had already been applied, if we consider some of the great performances of this century, like Edith Evans as Rebecca, Eva Le Gallienne as Hedda and Flora Robson as Mrs Alving. The truth seems to be that Ibsen's lines do embody characters who possess all the qualities and dimensions necessary to fashion a great individual performance. We are in an especially good position today to verify the enduring elements in Ibsen's characterization, since we are sufficiently remote from most of the limiting social concerns of his first audiences, which made sinners of Nora and Mrs Alving, and saints of Torvald, Parson Manders and Gregers Werle of *The Wild Duck.*

Ibsen's art was soon to pass from his plays of social realism to those of a more symbolic vision, from *The Wild Duck* to *Rosmersholm* and *Hedda Gabler.* Even greater demands were placed upon the acting skills of those who played Rebecca and Hedda. Ibsen's power of communicating further subtleties of the unspoken grew with his ability to explore human relationships and to convey increasing suggestions of the irrational. Conflicts seemed more allegorical, and whole characters existed on his stage only in a symbolic mode. But thus far it can be said that, in the development of dramatic art, Ibsen has been an outstanding example of a writer setting the pace for the modern actor and director. All the more so because by the turn of the century he had become a figure of world importance.

5 Realism in France: Antoine and the Théâtre-Libre

André Antoine (1858—1943) carried the banner for Zola and Ibsen in France. In 1887, this unknown gas company clerk and a group of amateur players opened their Théâtre-Libre with four modest one-act plays, one of which was a dramatization of Zola's story *Jacques Damour*. Antoine launched his theatre by subscription, collecting 3,500 francs for the first season; of this, some 1,000 francs were paid out for a place to rehearse, and he took some rehearsals in a bar in the Rue Lepic. To make up the sets, he carried the furniture from his mother's house (it is still the common practice among amateurs to bring their own props), and friends delivered the invitations to the theatre by hand in order to save postage. But soon the theatre was packed from floor to ceiling for every performance, with the result that the subscription for the second season was 40,000 francs and Antoine was able to buy the scenery and pay his actors.

The theatre itself was little more than an obscure wooden hall up a flight of steps at the end of an alley, the Passage de l'Élysée des Beaux Arts. It seated only 343 people and was equipped with a miniature stage that suited the small scale of the settings in the plays Antoine chose. In his *Impressions de théâtre*, Jules Lemaître, the leading critic of the Paris theatre, reported doubtfully on its size:

> One might stretch out one's hand to the actors over the foot-lights and put one's legs on the prompter's box. The stage is so narrow that only the most elementary scenery can be used on it, and it is so near to us that scenic illusion is impossible.

An exceptional challenge to the realist was already present in such a theatre.

The Théâtre-Libre was the first of Europe's modern laboratory theatres, and the system of paying its way by subscription sales had the incidental virtue of compelling the audience to share in the experiment of testing new methods and new material on the stage. In the seven years that followed, Antoine explored the art of natural-istic acting and directing to an extent which the Meiningen company had never done, and although his aims were not exclus-ively naturalistic, he supplied a stage in the world's dramatic capital for the magic new names of the realistic movement: Tolstoy (*The Power of Darkness*, produced 1888), Ibsen (*Ghosts*, 1890 and *The Wild Duck*, 1891), Strindberg (*Miss Julie*, 1893) and Hauptmann (*The Weavers*, also 1893).

The Power of Darkness had been banned in Russia, but for the Théâtre-Libre its production was the most important event of the first season. Tolstoy's grim play dealt with the degradation of the Russian peasantry and the growth of the riminal impulse. Dumas, Augier, Sardou and the well-known critic Francisque Sarcey had all found the play too sombre, and had advised against producing it. As it turned out, Antoine's production was a triumph. The *Revue des Deux Mondes* reported,

> It was Austerlitz. When the curtain came down in a tempest
> of applause on the final scene, the audience was enraptured.
> I never noticed an instant of relaxation or inattention during
> the whole four hours... For the first time a setting and
> costumes truly borrowed from the daily customs of Russian
> life appeared on the French stage without comic opera
> embellishments and without that predilection for tinsel and
> falsity which seems inherent in our theatrical atmosphere.

After this, the name of the Théâtre-Libre reverberated round Europe.

Antoine's production of *Ghosts* was the first recorded produc-tion of any play by Ibsen in France. It had previously been the opening shot fired in the campaign of Berlin's Freie Bühne and London's Independent Theatre. Artistic and literary Paris was in the stalls and boxes, reported George Moore in *Impressions and Opinions*, and the larger Théâtre des Menus Plaisirs, taken for the occasion, was filled to capacity. However, the French considered the play to be only a 'brilliant failure'. They were not worried by the moral issues of the play, but they found Ibsen aloof and obscure, even boring. He was 'a Zola with a wooden leg', lacking in French clarity,

5. Ibsen, *The Wild Duck*, 1891. Production by André Antoine at the Théâtre-Libre, Paris.

with none of the expected points and arguments coming through explicitly. But not all French critics agreed, and Jules Lemaître thought the play 'a beautiful and strong tragedy', and Paul Desjardins considered Ibsen 'the greatest living dramatist' on the strength of this production. It was the foreigner George Moore who had least trouble with the play, and he commented on 'the remorseless web that life had spun, and the poor boy entangled in it'. When Oswald, played by Antoine himself, asked that his mother poison him, he felt the terror 'moving among the spectators' to be unbearable, and found the 'nervous irritation of the sick man' to be 'faultlessly rendered', and the scene in which Mrs Alving sees Oswald kiss Regina to be 'so supremely awful, so shockingly true'.

Nevertheless, *Ghosts* was pronounced a failure, and the more enigmatic *Wild Duck*, according to Sarcey, a bigger failure still. Of all these mountains, only *The Weavers* appeared to have been scaled with any success, when it was reported in Antoine's *Souvenirs sur le Théâtre-Libre* that the overrunning of the manufacturer's home in the fourth act brought the whole house to its feet in terror. But Antoine could not accept the general judgment on Ibsen. Playing Oswald, he had had a new experience as an actor, he said, 'an almost complete loss of my own personality.' We may interpret for better or worse the interesting reaction he had then: 'After the second act I remembered nothing, neither the audience nor the effect of the production, and, shaking and weakened, I was some time getting hold of myself again after the final curtain had fallen' (translated M. A. Carlson).

In 1897 Antoine became the director of the Théâtre Antoine, and he made it the headquarters for all the young enthusiasts of the new drama. Finally, in 1906, he was honoured with an appointment as director of the Odéon. He was France's first *metteur en scène*, was the first to make amateur acting a respectable activity in France, and began the process of breaking down the star system, which he saw as one of the greatest obstacles to the development of the drama in Paris.

Antoine flew in the face of the established acting style of the Paris Conservatoire, the acting school of the Comédie-Française and the classical French theatre as a whole, which he believed had paralysed the profession. The classical French actor was encouraged

to develop a 'type' to fill the needs of the repertory; he was trained
in the art of elocution and was accustomed to 'recite' his part rather
then live it, declaiming his lines and emphasizing key words rather
than talking naturally; he would use the same gestures whatever his character; he would never speak when he moved; and he
was expected to master this and a hundred other rules. As a result
of Antoine's attack on the accepted ways, his actor now seemed unconscious of the presence of his audience, he acted with his whole
body, not just with voice and gesture. Antoine never allowed him to
break character by glancing at the prompter, striking a pose
or playing for effect; and he was prepared to vary his performance
to meet the requirements of each individualized part. He used
natural gestures and seemed to behave as in ordinary life, even
to the point of acting with his back to the audience: indeed, the
Théâtre-Libre was lightly referred to as 'the theatre of Antoine's
Back', and one wag suggested that a rich uncle had threatened to cut
Antoine out of his will if he ever saw him on the stage.

As a director, Antoine believed in perfecting the slightest
detail of speech, gesture and stage business, and he worked to
synthesize their effect. 'Returning a pencil or tipping over a cup',
he said, 'will be as significant and will have as profound an effect
on the mind of the audience as the grandiloquent excesses of the
romantic theatre.' He believed in rehearsing his actors as an
ensemble, working with real furniture and real props. He felt that
the director's contribution had to be one of infinite care and
patience, all to deceive an audience into thinking that what it saw
was actuality.

He became especially well-known for his stage settings. They
aimed at a perfect picture of life: in the enduring slogan of one of the
leading young playwrights, Jean Jullien, it was to be a *tranche de vie*,
a 'slice of life'. The scene was to be as if set in a room with its fourth
wall removed, and in an article 'Causerie sur la mise en scène' which
he wrote for *La Revue de Paris* of 1 April 1903, Antoine explained:

> For a stage set to be original, striking and authentic, it should
> first be built in accordance with something seen —whether a
> landscape or an interior. If it is an interior, it should be built
> with its four sides, its four walls, without worrying about the
> fourth wall, which will later disappear so as to enable the
> audience to see what is going on. (Translated J.M. Bernstein.)

Here now was another basic theory of the naturalistic drama, developed from Ibsen: the idea of the 'fourth wall'. An interior set should be designed as if the room were part of a whole house, with a ceiling, or beams, overhead to lend it solidity. The designer should then fill his stage with a great number of small props to give it the feeling of being lived in. It had to be a facsimile of the real thing. Antoine eventually rejected footlights, as Zola and Strindberg had suggested earlier: 'In life light comes from above, not from below.'

The principle behind this unusual emphasis on the scene was simply explained. If the environment was essential to the naturalism which inspired the new drama, then the immediate setting in which its characters lived and moved was equally important. So it was that Antoine gradually came to create his stage settings first, taking rehearsals on a stage already set, so that the setting should partly determine the behaviour of the characters. He considered that the secret of his early success lay in his scene design, and it is easy to see how his sets became fascinating to look at in themselves.

While he was at the Odéon, Antoine attempted to apply his new stage philosophy, not only to the realistic plays of the new movement, but also to the classics, Aeschylus, Sophocles, Shakespeare, Calderón, Racine, Molière, Goethe and Schiller. He claimed that his object was not to rejuvenate their plays by modernizing their staging, so much as to present them as if in their own period with more simple and appropriate sets. He was fond of quoting Molière's assertion that it was important to 'act as one speaks', and he believed that to act a formal classic like Racine with a natural simplicity would have the effect of moving an audience more than before. This idea of treating the classics as if they were contemporary has in fact been taken up everywhere in this century, to the delight of some and the indignation of others.

Antoine's productions became famous, but his final claim to fame lay in his encouragement of a host of new playwrights. Through him, Paris was able to see the psychological drama of François de Curel, the problem plays of Giovanni Verga, the later work of Henry Becque and the comedies of Georges de Porto-Riche. But of all Antoine's protégés, Eugène Brieux was the most immediately successful. With a characteristic flourish, Bernard Shaw once said of him 'Europe has today a Sophocles in the person of Eugène Brieux.' Shaw was referring to Brieux's notorious play *Les Avariés* (*Damaged Goods*), which strips its respectable bourgeois hero, M. Loches, of his illusions, just as Sophocles stripped Oedipus, and rattled a few less classical skeletons in their closet. Shaw thought Brieux the natural successor to Ibsen, in fact, and paid tribute to his 'scientific spirit' in his preface to *Three Plays by Brieux* (1911). What perhaps chiefly appealed to Shaw was Brieux's repeated challenge to the French censor by his treatment on the public stage of every taboo subject: syphilis, dowry marriages, abortion, birth control, prostitution and more, but Antoine himself thought all this a little too ingeniously amoral. As it happened, Brieux's didacticism rendered his plays obsolete rather quickly. It is a truth that nothing is more second-rate than second-rate naturalism.

6 *Strindberg's contribution to realism*

The Father (1887), *Miss Julie* (1888)

Up to a point the playwriting career of Johan August Strindberg (1849–1912) runs parallel to Ibsen's. Strindberg's early plays were romantic historical dramas in the fashion of the time. In 1884 he even wrote two plays called *Getting Married*, with a preface on women's and men's rights, as a riposte to *A Doll's House*; as a result of this, he was tried on grounds of immorality before being acquitted. Then, like Ibsen, he startled the Scandinavian public with two plays of such uncompromising realism that those who followed the naturalistic movement in Europe decided that another leader had arrived. These plays, however, were still written partly in reaction against Ibsen's feminism, although they had distinctive contributions to make to naturalism on the stage. They were *The Father* (1887) and *Miss Julie* (1888), each characteristically dashed off in less than two weeks. To these should be added *Creditors* (also 1888), written in about a month. But already the realism in these plays contained within itself the seeds of its own dissolution, so that the achievements of Strindberg's later years, from *To Damascus* (1898) and *A Dream Play* (1902) to *The Ghost Sonata* (1907) and the other 'chamber' plays, are so frankly experimental and unrealistic that the playwright earns another place as an expressionist. Always restless in his search for an appropriate form for his themes, in his time Strindberg wrote sixty-two plays, and in so doing created an astonishing number of dramatic modes and techniques which dominated the western theatre of the twentieth century.

Strindberg was an acute analyst of the French naturalistic school which immediately preceded him. He was aware of the originality of Zola's *Thérèse Raquin*, and saw that it was far more than a thesis play. Where Dumas and Augier would probably have made Thérèse's murder of her husband an occasion for attacking the divorce laws, Zola had focused upon Thérèse's motives, probed her mind and studied the consequences of her action. But did Zola dig deeply enough? 'In the pangs of conscience of the criminals', Strindberg wrote, '[Zola] sees merely an expression of disrupted social harmony, the results of habit and inherited ideas.' He particularly noted that the lapse of a year after the murder cost the play its unity and intensity of illusion. The necessity of unity and illusion would occupy Strindberg's attention all his life. He also warned against the danger of triviality: mere realism of the surface was 'photography which includes everything, even the grain of dust on the lens of the camera'. Good naturalism, on the other hand, looked for the natural conflicts where the crucial struggles were: true naturalism sought out the points where the great battles occurred to have his own plays deal in fundamental truths, like those of the sexual relationship, the psychological conflict of wills and the bearing of the past on the present.

Antoine's Théâtre-Libre set him an impressive example. Strindberg admired the simplicity of its settings, which were quite unlike those of the commercial theatre. Dazzling sets, he believed, were designed to deceive the audience into thinking a play better than it was. A table and two chairs were all that were needed to present 'the most powerful conflicts life had to offer'. He also approved Antoine's choice of one-act plays, because they afforded that desirable unity of time and place. And he approved a repertoire which rejected the old plots of devious intrigue, preferring the psychological examination of character as it underwent the basic struggles — for subsistence, for love or honour or freedom, for life itself. At the Théâtre-Libre, Strindberg recognized, the new writer had an opportunity to explore new themes, new forms.

Hostility greeted both of Strindberg's great plays of naturalism. *The Father* could not open in Sweden, and *Miss Julie* waited sixteen years for a production there. Because of the censor, the first production of the latter was a single private performance in the Student Union of Copenhagen University in 1889 with Strindberg's wife Siri von Essen as Julie. There was not another until 1892, when Otto Brahm also had a single performance at his Freie Bühne in Berlin. Its first extended production was not until 1893, when Antoine did it in French. Its first Swedish production was in 1904, but in another private performance, this time at Uppsala University. The full Swedish text did not reach the stage until 1949, when Alf Sjöberg restored the words cut by the censor, in a production at the Royal Dramatic Theatre in Stockholm.

The Father was an intimate study of a marital relationship, a bitter fight between the Captain, a man losing his mind and his integrity, and Laura, the woman who tortures him with the doubt that he is not the father of his child; Nietzsche agreed with the young author that a state of war between the sexes was a fundamental law of life and marriage. Strindberg intended the play to be his *Agamemnon*, the tragedy of the Greek king who fell victim to his wife's hatred, and it is true that in its classical economy and headlong rush to the final moment when the Captain is cajoled into a straitjacket, *The Father* is unlike other naturalistic plays. It is even arguable that the Captain and Laura are hardly individualized at all, but are simply representative of the male and the female principles. Moreover, the play actually needs none of the external detail of realism to make its point, and in the last analysis it can be played on a bare stage with only two props, the burning lamp thrown at the wife and the jacket put on the man. Strindberg seemed to be testing his principle of 'a table and two chairs'. The play becomes a starkly symbolic representation of the sexes in elemental conflict, and its form is already showing signs of Strindberg's future forays into the mode of expressionism. A real room is not needed to convey the battle of the sexes, and for all its realistic detail, even *Miss Julie* has been performed as a ballet, possibly the most abstract of dramatic forms.

Zola found *The Father* too abstract and calculated, and after its poor reception, Strindberg felt compelled to write a defence of his technique. In 1888 he therefore published a Foreword to *Miss Julie*, and this essay, which is as much an apologia for *The Father* as an introduction to *Miss Julie*, not only became a manifesto for the naturalistic movement, but also a remarkable document in the history of modern drama. In the *Drama Review* of winter 1968, Evert Sprinchorn suggested that there was not an idea in it that did not derive from the French thinking of the time, but no one had so completely synthesized the objectives, theoretical and technical, of the new movement.

Strindberg recognized that his new wine had burst the old bottles, and his Foreword took on the appearance of a prospectus. At the centre of his theory was his sense of character as an infinitely complicated thing only to be brought to life by granting it a large variety of motives for every action:

> In real life an action — this, by the way, is a somewhat new discovery — is generally caused by a whole series of motives, more or less fundamental, but as a rule the spectator chooses just one of these — the one which his mind can most easily grasp or that does most credit to his intelligence. A suicide is committed. Business troubles, says the man of affairs. Unrequited love, say the women. Sickness, says the invalid. Despair, says the down-and-out. But it is possible that the motive lay in all or none of these directions, or that the dead man concealed his actual motive by revealing quite another, likely to reflect more to his glory. (Translated Elizabeth Sprigge.)

So Strindberg explained that Julie's actions were motivated by her birth and upbringing, by the manner of the servant who seduced her, by the occasion of Midsummer Eve, and many other things all at work together.

Perhaps following the French psychologists Ribot and Charcot, as suggested by B. G. Madsen in *Strindberg's Naturalistic Theatre*, but long before the impact of Freud, Strindberg believed that as a naturalist he should make what he called the 'soul-complex' of a character rich with the effects on the mind of past and present events. In theory, none of this implied a moral or didactic position by the dramatist, although it is hard for us not to regard some of Julie's motives as the result of her author's own anti-feminism. In his review of *The Father*, Jules Lemaître had thought he recognized in Strindberg 'un misogyne éminent', and in fact Strindberg complained of the performance of Julie by his wife Siri von Essen because she played it like a martyr and not an emancipated man-hater.

However, what is outstanding in the play is not the mystery of Julie's sex drives, or the urge of Jean the valet to rise above his class, which in any case Strindberg admired, but the way these combine. The hidden structure of the play, emerging through detail and tone, is based upon the special relationship between class and sex. 'Sexually', Strindberg wrote, '[Jean] is the aristocrat because of his virility'; Julie may be mistress in the class struggle, but Jean is master in the sex war. Thus one pattern is imposed ironically upon another, and in fact reinforces it, a sexual motive informing and revealing a social phenomenon in a way attempted again only in Jean Genêt's *Le Balcon* in 1957, where sexual fantasies are seen as the sensational extensions of established social institutions.

Strindberg had other important things to say in his Foreword. He claimed that he had avoided the mechanical question-and-answer regularity of dialogue found in the French romantic drama, and that he had instead allowed his dialogue to meander, or seem to do so, with one speaker engaging the mind of another as if by chance; themes would be repeated and developed 'as in a musical composition'. Now this method of composing the lines nicely describes what Chekhov achieved ten years later, and perhaps the sexual evasions and hidden aggressions are of this order in the first scene of *Miss Julie*, especially when the cook Kristin is present with Julie and Jean to inhibit the expression of what they really mean. But it is noticeable that Strindberg's 'subtextual' kind of dialogue at the beginning of the play changes radically once the seduction is completed and there is nothing more to hide. It is then that the dialogue becomes explicit and ceases to meander. Thus as Julie grows conscious of her humiliation, so she falls to her knees, clasps her hands and cringes before Jean, who rises to stand triumphantly, and symbolically, over her. This manner derives from the old theatricality, as does the overt exchange of such lines as, 'Beast!' — 'Merde!' — 'Menial! Lackey!' — 'Menial's whore, lackey's harlot!' This kind of dialogue is also a retreat to the more sensational

6. Strindberg, *Miss Julie*, 1959 ballet production for Swedish television, scene i. Choreography by Birgit Cullberg, with Elsa-Marianne von Rosen and Mario Mengarelli.

language of Zola, and is perhaps only redeemed in the last minutes of the play when the stage action becomes frankly symbolic: Jean takes Julie's songbird out of its cage and proceeds to chop off its head; the Count's bell, mute upon the wall throughout the play, rings suddenly, and Jean hurriedly changes back into his livery; finally, he places his razor into Julie's hand, and as the sun rises she walks out to her death as in a hypnotic trance − an idea apparently borrowed from Bernheim's study of 1884, *De la suggestion*. By the fall of the curtain, the dialogue has entirely ceased to 'meander' realistically, and it is hard to recognize the play itself as a cornerstone of the naturalistic movement.

Strindberg advocated other techniques, all of which were to have strong repercussions in the modern theatre. He had avoided dividing his play into acts, he said, because he did not want any intervals to disturb 'the suggestive influence of the author-hypnotist', another notion picked up from Bernheim, and an argument which Bertolt Brecht would seize upon with derision. In order not to break the illusion, Strindberg also wanted to be rid of any musicians that the audience could see: it was Brecht again who later insisted that the musicians must be visible. Strindberg would not tolerate supper-parties or other such distracting elements common in the Victorian theatre, and demanded total blackout in the auditorium to make sure: Brecht was to advocate that the audience must be totally aware that it is in a theatre at all times. All of Strindberg's requirements for the intense concentration of the audience during performance clearly indicate his idea of dramatic illusion. His audience was to be completely convinced of the reality of the world of the stage, and transported wholly into its sphere of influence.

As for the stage setting for *Miss Julie*, Strindberg decided to show only part of the kitchen in which the action was to take place, and requested that what was seen should be arranged diagonally, in order that the spectator should complete what was not seen by visualizing it in his imagination. We may be excused today for observing first, however, the provocative aptness of choosing a kitchen as the place to degrade a lady of the upper-class. Then Strindberg also revealed that he had borrowed the idea of the asymmetry and economy of the scene from impressionist painting, another unmistakable hint of the future disintegration of the realistic mode of drama. He echoed a common cry of the time when he asked also for the kitchen shelves and utensils to be real props, and not just painted on the canvas backcloth. In addition, he called, like Antoine, for the footlights to be abolished, and again like Antoine, for the actors not to play to the audience. Actors should also abandon the convenience of acting downstage centre to be as near as possible to the prompter's box (downstage centre in the Victorian theatre) — although this was far from being a plea for underacting, which would have been contrary to the Swedish tradition. And Strindberg believed that the art of drama could develop and flourish only if the house and stage were smaller, a condition he managed to achieve in his own Dagmar Theatre in Copenhagen in 1888, modelled on Antoine's Théâtre-Libre. Later, his Intima Theatre in Stockholm was smaller still. In all, Strindberg's Foreword was a very remarkable document, one which anticipated in one department of theatre practice after another many basic changes in the twentieth century. Even Bernard Shaw asked that the set for the first act of *The Philanderer* (1893) not be rectangular.

His experimental theatre in Copenhagen failed, but, like Ibsen, Strindberg became a director of plays, and so had first-hand experience of the obstacles to realizing a realistic scene on the stage. But as he found that the reality he sought to express grew more complicated, he developed new techniques in writing and production which took him further away from the realism of the naturalistic movement. Indeed, Strindberg himself recognized the change to expressionism in his own work, and declared, 'To me falls the task of bridging the gap between naturalism and supra-naturalism by proclaiming that the latter is only a development of the former' (translated B. G. Madsen from the 1912 edition of Strindberg's works).

7 Realism in Germany: Brahm and Hauptmann

The Weavers (1892)

'We have erected a free stage for modern life', announced Otto Brahm (1856–1912). Inspired by Antoine's Théâtre-Libre, Brahm opened his Freie Bühne in Berlin in 1889, and his first production was predictably Ibsen's *Chosts*. Brahm had spent ten years as a scholarly critic for the *Vossische Zeitung* in Berlin, and was Germany's leading advocate of Zola, Ibsen and the naturalistic movement. The evangelical tone was heard again, and his manifesto began,

> Once upon a time there was an art which avoided the present and sought poetry only in the darkness of the past, striving in a bashful flight from reality to reach those ideal distant shores where in eternal youth there blooms what has never happened anywhere. The art of our time embraces, with its tentacles, everything that lives: nature and society; that is why the closest and subtlest relations bind modern art and modern life together; and anyone who wants to grasp modern art must endeavour to penetrate modern life as well in its thousand merging contours, in its intertwined and antagonistic instincts. The motto of this new art, written down in golden characters by our leading spirits, is one word — truth; and truth, truth on every path of life, is what we are striving for. Not the objective truth, which escapes the struggling individual, but individual truth, freely arrived at from the deepest convictions, freely uttered: the truth of the independent spirit who has nothing to explain away or hide; and who therefore knows only one adversary, his arch-enemy and mortal foe: the lie in all its forms. (Translated Martin Esslin.)

With the opening of the Freie Bühne, Brahm's theories of truth in drama, of honesty in acting and production, could be tested on a stage of his own. Unlike Antoine and his amateurs, Brahm was assisted by a number of well-established actors and directors, including the distinguished actor Emanuel Reicher. They all shared Brahm's convictions, and together they preached and practised a concept of drama based upon a richer, more penetrating representation of human beings on the stage. As with Antoine, this concept implied the rejection of the stereotype, the dialogue of tirade and bombast, the familiar gesture and the sonorous voice.

Brahm's major statement of theory, 'The Old and the New Art of Acting', focused on the essence of truth in performance. He suggested in his scholarly way that the new acting was no other than the traditional art of German acting, before that of the nineteenth century, and found it in the so-called 'Hamburg realists' of the low German style in the eighteenth century. Only when Goethe became artistic manager of the Weimar Court Theatre school of poetic drama, working with his own and Schiller's romantic dramas, did 'classicism' dominate the acting style of the German theatre. The classical actors spoke with emphatic, deep voices and moved with stylized, stiff gestures — offstage as well as on; measured tones and sculptured poses were *de rigueur*. Goethe, it is said, directed a play like the conductor of an orchestra or an opera, beating out the rhythm of the words with a baton. At its best, this style encouraged a poetic transfiguration of the stage, but in seeking universal truths in characterization, it unfortunately lost something of the required individuality of the person re-presented. The new actor, declared Brahm, was no antiquarian, and the living art of acting had to discard the classical rules if it was to survive: the actor had to return to a true observation of man and test his work in accordance with nature. He had perforce to see with contemporary eyes.

The Meiningen Company had created the realistic setting, but had failed to place realistic people in it. In looking for a model, therefore, Brahm cited the work of the early nineteenth-century French actor François Joseph Talma as an example of the reformed style he wanted. Talma had reduced the declamatory manner in tragedy, following the sense of the lines before their metre, playing to the others on the stage rather than to the audience, and even on occasion turning his back on them, a practice abhorred by his contemporary, Goethe, as lack of restraint. This feature Brahm considered to be symbolic of the new acting. Turning one's back represented the difference between truth and convention in performance, and it was this that his critics, like Karl Frenzel, found just as 'ugly' as Goethe had.

Brahm made another point. He believed that historically the creative arts had an inner kinship with the performing arts: the two influenced each other and developed in parallel. If exaggerated effects in painting and playwriting had been infused with genuine feeling, the actor could not long stay out of step with his fellow artists. But revolutions in a multi-art form like that of the theatre are not easy. Antoine had created his own company out of his amateurs, training them himself in his own ways. Brahm's professionals, however, proved more reluctant to form a true ensemble devoted to naturalism, and he ran into the typical conflict which arises from any attempt to change theatre practice too quickly. When, for example, he tried to direct an actor of the old school like Josef Kainz, a performer greatly admired for the extraordinary grace of his speech and movement, Kainz's own concern for 'harmony' in word and action inevitably contradicted the psychological realism Brahm wanted.

Another typical conflict arose when Brahm was officially recognized and appointed director of the Deutsches Theater in 1894. Like Antoine at the Odéon, Brahm immediately wished to apply his new methods to the classics, while preserving the inner mood and spirit of the originals. This is a policy towards the classics of western drama which the twentieth century has never ceased to pursue, always with uncertain results. Brahm believed that the classics had to live and change with their audiences, on the assumption that although a play may be old, the art of drama is always new and immediate. The production of Sophocles's *Antigone* at the Deutsches Theater, for example, carefully avoided the traditional proscenium setting for a Greek tragedy, the symmetrical platform with colonnade, which was thought to be the rough equivalent of the ancient Greek *proskenion*. Brahm instead constructed asymmetrical wing-pieces and had the acting space divided into two, with steps linking further acting areas upstage and downstage. Decorated with trees and tapestries, the new palace began to look positively lived-in. In addition, the chorus no longer assembled formally around the altar, but moved freely about and spoke from one side. It was quite a domesticated group of Theban nobles, even if Mendelssohn's music had the effect of making them somewhat like a chorus from grand opera.

The source of Brahm's greatest dissatisfaction with the old methods lay in the traditional way of acting. He had chosen the *Antigone* for its ageless theme, the conflict between the needs of society and the rights of the individual, but in Brahm's view, Creon remained too cold and symbolic a figure, and not sufficiently moving as a portrait of a fallen ruler. Yet any step Brahm tried to take towards making a great impersonal tragedy appear more realistic was of course strictly limited by the nature of the original. Antigone and Ismene also played too statuesquely, lacking the individuality he sought, and only the smaller parts of the Watchman and Haemon seemed in any sense human. The truth was that Brahm's realism was not suited to the exalted language of tragedy, and even less to the stylized comedy of the past. Every time the Deutsches Theater played the classics, the actors were torn between two masters, the author and the director.

Brahm's greatest achievement, like Antoine's, was to introduce new playwrights to his own audience, among them Ibsen and Strindberg, but especially Gerhart Hauptmann (1862–1946). Their plays presented the customary challenge to the authorities, and the sale of subscriptions was adopted as a way of avoiding the censor, although it was unfortunate that such subscriptions restricted the audiences of the Freie Bühne to those from the middle-classes. It fell to the more radical Bruno Wille to open his Freie Volksbühne in 1890, and then his Neue Freie Bühne in 1892, offering seats at lower prices in order to appeal to a wider group of play-goers. It would be naive to assume that naturalism was the art form of the working-classes at this time, but the German theatre as a source of social consciousness certainly begins with Otto Brahm.

The Freie Bühne opened its second season with a play designed to stun and scandalize the audience: Hauptmann's *Vor Sonnenaufgang* (*Before Sunrise*, 1889), strongly influenced by Tolstoy's squalid scene in *The Power of Darkness*. It is a gloomy play of brutal realism; its subject is the effect of alcoholism on the poor, and among other things manages to include incestuous bestiality: the objective critic might well have asked whether life was always so unrelievedly black. With act II, the house was in an uproar, and in act V, in which a baby is noisily delivered offstage, a pair of delivery forceps was hurled on to the stage. In the character of the agitator Alfred Loth, the play appeared to demand social reform, all the more urgently because of the suffering of the pathetic heroine Helena Krause. But in many eyes, the use of the stage for social criticism was a gross abuse, and had turned the theatre into 'a cess-pit'. At all events, it is easy to see why this production is thought to be the one which brought in the German naturalistic movement, although not easy to imagine an audience today so prepared to get into a fight over a matter of aesthetic theory.

No play, however, better exemplifies the new direction of the realistic theatre than Hauptmann's *Die Weber* (*The Weavers*, 1892). This was his most notorious naturalistic piece, a play with a wholly political object. It dealt with the unsuccessful revolt of the Silesian weavers in 1844; Hauptmann was the grandson of a Silesian

7. Hauptmann, *The Weavers*, 1894. Poster.

weaver, and so wrote from the heart. It was particularly pertinent since Silesia had suffered a famine in 1890, and Hauptmann had visited the region in 1891 to see the piece-workers in their hovels, and witness their squalor and starvation for himself. In *The Weavers*, therefore, a playwright had dared to apply the principles of authenticity for the first time to history, treating his subject as if it were contemporary. Today we should label such a piece 'dramatized documentary'.

The story of the early production of the play is one of constant battle with the censorship, due entirely to its *Tendenz*, its intention to advance a social cause, preach a social message, which was considered to be socialistic. At first, its author had tried to have it produced at the Deutsches Theater, but it was banned 'for police reasons connected with public order'; the complaint was that it had been written in the Silesian dialect so that the weavers could understand its incendiary meaning. When it was rewritten in High German in 1893, it was banned again, the complaint then being that the general public would be able to understand it. It met similar opposition elsewhere, and it was not presented in Austria until 1903, or in Russia until 1904. It was, however, received enthusias-

8. Hauptmann, *The Weavers*, 1894. Production by Otto Brahm at the Freie Buhne, Berlin. Act v.

tically at the Freie Bühne in 1894, with thunderous applause after each act; when the mob plundered the manufacturer's drawing-room, it was encouraged by shouts from the audience to do so more vigorously.

The Weavers took on a different appearance from Ibsen's social plays, which by comparison seemed to be plays of argument between three or four characters. In his play, Hauptmann introduced some forty named parts, all speaking in dialect, to depict the nature of mass hunger and universal poverty. He saw his weavers as a group, and the critics were quick to seize the point that the play had no hero in the usual sense, only a 'collective hero', the masses themselves. Hauptmann spoke of himself as a biologist: his object, he said, was to report the truth accurately, and to prompt compassion for the suffering of an actual social group. In this, *The Weavers* anticipated Gorky's *The Lower Depths* (1902), and provided a model for O'Neill's *The Iceman Cometh* (1946).

The effect of a crowd of characters on the stage can be foggy, and the action of the play shapeless, but Hauptmann worked out his material in a mosaic of fine detail, and developed his picture so that it changed with the passage of time without the need for a plot of the old kind. He explained that his drama was 'not so much the ready-made result of thought as the *thinking process* itself'. This notion will emerge again in Brecht's idea of a play as a dialectic designed to make an audience discuss the issues with itself and with the actors as it proceeds. The locations in *The Weavers* pass from the textile factory where the weavers try to sell their work, to the miserable home of one of the workers, then to a tavern, then to the employer's house where the riot begins, and finally, as the revolt spreads, to a room in another weaver's hovel in another village. The shifting scene and the many different people supply a description of a social condition, and make a total statement like a moving picture.

Already another new principle was at work in the German independent theatre. Writing in the *Drama Review* for winter 1968, Martin Esslin suggested that naturalism acknowledged 'the primacy of content over form': the drama was capable of expressing in stage action any material drawn from life, whether dealing with social and political issues or conveying the subjective urges of the

human spirit. The playwright had only to find the dramatic mode
and shape best suited to his subject and purpose: 'Artistic form thus
came to be seen as the *organic expression* of its content.' The truth of
this is probably impossible to prove or to disprove, but as a principle it may account for the striking fact that each of the great
naturalists, Ibsen, Strindberg, Hauptmann and Chekhov, very soon
after writing a successful play in the realistic mode, felt the need to
write some other way.

8 *Realism in Britain: Archer and Grein*

Some time before Ibsen took Europe by storm, domestic realism had
made modest progress in the London theatre on its own. T. W.
Robertson (1829—71) wrote social comedies which seem unaccept-
ably sentimental and melodramatic now, but his gently satirical
view of English middle- and upper-class society, together with
unaccustomed glimpses of the Victorian working-class, placed him
well ahead of his time. He wrote a sequence of plays with social
themes for the Prince of Wales's Theatre, plays which advertised
themselves by their aggressively staccato one-word titles, *Society*
(1865), *Ours* (1866) and *Caste* (1867). In *Plays and Controversies*, Yeats
condemned Tom Robertson to oblivion by saying that he reflected
only the surface of life:

> The author of *Caste* made a reputation by putting what
> seemed to be average common life and average common
> speech for the first time upon the stage in England, and
> by substituting real loaves of bread and real cups of tea
> for imaginary ones (p. 155).

No doubt Yeats's summary judgment has coloured our view of
Robertson's achievement, even though Yeats's attacks on the
naturalistic movement were commonplace.

In common with his age, Robertson was a moralist, but he

showed some signs of wanting to *demonstrate* his moral points in the modern way, rather than merely utter moral sentiments about the acquisitive society and the barriers of class. *Caste*, for example, examined the difficulties of Esther Eccles, a working-class girl married to a man from the upper-classes, George D'Alroy. But the play also provided explicitly English points of reference by introducing the girl's drunken father, her sister Polly and Polly's friend Sam Gerridge, a plumber — all present in order to expand the simple contrast between the world of poor Esther and the snobbery of the D'Alroy family. Like his fellows on the Continent, Robertson also attacked the old theatricalism, and was taken with the idea of bringing realism to the scenery and the dialogue as well as to the plot. His disciple of the next generation, Arthur Wing Pinero, depicted Robertson in the character of the penurious author Tom Wrench in *Trelawny of the Wells*, struggling to have his new style of playwriting recognized: 'I strive to make my people talk and behave like people', he explains, 'to fashion heroes out of actual, dull, everyday men, and heroines from simple maidens in muslin frocks.' Almost a Chekhovian sentiment.

Robertson died before he could know of Ibsen's work, but Ibsen found an early advocate in Britain in Edmund Gosse (1849–1928), whose writing for *The Spectator*, *The Academy*, *Fraser's Magazine* and *The Fortnightly Review* in the years 1872 and 1873 brought the first important British recognition of the new writer from Scandinavia. Like many academics after him, Gosse taught himself Norwegian in order to read Ibsen in the original. He reviewed the *Poems*, and thereafter began to review the plays, qualifying himself as Ibsen's champion in Britain. At first Gosse regarded Ibsen as a satirical and poetic dramatist, basing his judgment on *The League of Youth*, *Brand* and *Peer Gynt*, but his interest in him dwindled with the passing of the earlier poetic dramas and the coming of the realistic social plays, which Gosse found pessimistic. In his way, he anticipated the far-reaching conflict between writers of *l'art pour l'art*, 'art for art's sake', and the socially committed, a conflict which dominated much of the first half of the twentieth century. Luckily for Ibsen and the new movement in Britain, another champion came forward at the right time.

The Scottish critic William Archer (1856–1924) took up

Ibsen's cause where Gosse dropped it. Archer had an advantage
in that he had grown up in Norway and spoke the language fluently,
and he promoted Ibsen in the most direct way possible, by trans-
lating him, by helping his plays on to the London stage and by an
enthusiastic stream of technical commentary on the new drama. His
best book, *The Old Drama and the New* (1923), for all it is wrong-
headed in its enthusiasm some of the time, is a competent reassessment of the history of drama in the light of Ibsen's achievement, and
it confidently places him among the very great. But Archer was also
interested in the theatre *per se*, and in an unusual study of the art
of acting, *Masks or Faces?* (1880), he curiously anticipates Stanislavsky's assessment of the imaginative sympathy required of an
actor who wishes to embrace his part completely.

The first production of Ibsen in London, an adaptation of
The Pillars of Society in 1880, was the result of two years of effort by
Archer; the play was given a single matinée performance at the
Gaiety Theatre under the Robertsonian title of *Quicksands*. The
production caused scarcely a ripple, although when the audience
called for the new author, the young William Archer did not hesitate
to step out and take a bow. From that time, he became Ibsen's self-
appointed guardian in English, and nothing escaped him. Elizabeth
Robins, who created the first Hedda in English, recalled his 'standing
guard over Ibsen's interests at every rehearsal', and with notebook at
the ready, he was 'a kind of Recording Angel setting down our sins of
omission and commission'. For the next few years Archer continued
to write ceaselessly of Ibsen's work, pointing to his force as a realist,
praising his rejection of facile idealism, naming him with consider-
able foresight as 'one of the great negative voices of a negative age'
in the *St James's Magazine* of January 1881.

In that year also, there occurred the important meeting
between Archer and one George Bernard Shaw. This took place in
the vast Reading Room of the British Museum Library, where
Archer found Shaw 'alternately, if not simultaneously' poring over
Karl Marx's *Das Kapital* in French and an orchestral score of Wagner's
Tristan und Isolde. The two were of the same age, twenty-five, and
their common interest in Ibsen and the new drama dates from soon
after that chance encounter.

By 1889, some of Archer's translations of Ibsen's plays had

been published, and in that year *A Doll's House* in his translation was given its first London production at the Novelty Theatre, Kingsway. This production marked the first formal recognition of Ibsen in the English theatre, a rumbling prelude to the explosion which would be heard three years later when *Ghosts* was performed. *A Doll's House* was generally condemned as dreary, with the note of authenticity in the dialogue coming, if anything, as an unwelcome shock, and Ibsen's unheroic characters failing to tempt a digestion sated for years with romantic melodrama. Clement Scott's abusive attacks on Ibsen began with this production, and subscribers to *The Theatre* were startled to read on 1 July 1889,

> The atmosphere is hideous ... it is all self, self, self! ... a congregation of men and women without one spark of nobility in their nature, men without conscience and women without affection, an unlovable, unlovely and detestable crew.

The familiar complaint that Ibsen was 'morbid and unwholesome' began to be heard that summer. There was an inept production of *Rosmersholm* at the Vaudeville in February, and then the storm broke with the London production of *Ghosts* in March 1891. In his biography of Ibsen, Michael Meyer suggested that this production was 'as controversial and epoch-making as the first night of Victor Hugo's *Hernani* or Synge's *The Playboy of the Western World*'.

With this production of *Ghosts*, the story is taken up by another pioneer, Jacob Grein (1862–1935), a young Dutchman who became a naturalized British subject in 1895. Working in London and writing occasional dramatic criticism, his desk became a natural venue for the exchange of plays between London and the Continent. Grein was determined to give London its Théâtre-Libre and its Freie Bühne, and in 1891, with just £80 in his pocket, he founded the Independent Theatre Society with the explicit intention of putting on 'plays which have a literary and artistic rather than a commercial value'. Parodying Grein's expected critics, Archer queried, 'Who is this Dutchman who dares to be dissatisfied with our honest, healthy, comfortable, fat and flourishing drama?', and indeed, Grein's first offering, *Ghosts*, was the one play wholly unacceptable to the commercial theatre or the Lord Chamberlain. The

Society was to be financed by subscription and present its plays in rented theatres. Like George Moore, who had written a relentless article on 'The Necessity of an English Théâtre-Libre', Grein believed that the long runs of the West End theatre made the production of experimental drama impossible. In all this Grein had the vigorous support of Archer and Shaw.

Grein's production of *Ghosts* received only one public dress rehearsal and one performance at the Royalty Theatre, but the roar of vituperative criticism was enough to secure Ibsen a name in Britain, and draw attention to Grein and the new drama as no praise could have done. Clement Scott's accusations in *The Daily Telegraph* of 14 March 1891 of 'a dirty act done publicly' were a fine advertisement for the struggling society, and in the *Fortnightly Review* that November Archer declared,

> I can call to mind no other case in literary history of a
> dramatist attaining such sudden and widespread notoriety
> in a foreign country... This was the first time for half a
> century (to keep well within the mark) that a serious
> literary interest has also been primarily a theatrical interest.

Some few, however, saw more in *Ghosts* than a blinding insult; in particular, as we saw, A. B. Walkley found a spiritual quality in the play's revolt against conventional morality. But the general play-going public hereafter associated a naturalistic play, especially one from abroad, with outrage and scandal in some form or other.

The Independent Theatre Society battled on against popular opposition for six more years, until it finally ceased activity in 1897. It presented a *Thérèse Raquin* in 1891 and a notable *Wild Duck* in 1894. It was also responsible in its time for bringing the new symbolism to London, when in 1895 Grein invited Lugné-Poe to present not only Ibsen's *Rosmersholm* and *The Master Builder*, but also Maeterlinck's *L'Intruse* (*The Intruder*) and *Pelléas et Mélisande* in French. More than this, it showed the way for a host of other societies which sprang up in Britain in the early twentieth century. In 1921, Shaw wrote to Grein,

> When the papers ... declared that the manager of the
> theatre ought to be prosecuted for keeping a disorderly
> house, and that you and the foreign blackguard named

Ibsen who was your accomplice, should be deported as obvious undesirables, you made a hole in the dyke; and the weight of the flood outside did the rest.

According to his memoirs, Grein said he was content to be the one who had made the hole: 'In letting Ibsen in, I let the ocean in.' It was of greatest importance that new scripts began to flow, with Grein reading as many as ten a week. He was of course looking for the English Ibsen.

He did not find quite what he wanted. The English Ibsen was not an Englishman, but an Irishman. Nor was he the sober social reformer, but a witty social critic and a comedian of the first order. The young Bernard Shaw was waiting his chance.

9 *Shaw's contribution to realism*

Mrs Warren's Profession (1893), *Arms and the Man* (1894)

J. T. Grein approached George Bernard Shaw (1856—1950) with an invitation to try his hand at writing a realistic play for the Independent Theatre Society. As it happened, Shaw had attempted a play seven years before — he had collaborated with William Archer in 1885, but the authors had fallen out over the plot. The original preface to *Widowers' Houses* tells the amusing story of this collaboration, or rather contract, since Archer was to supply the plot and Shaw the dialogue. Archer carefully worked out the plan for the whole play along the correct 'well-made' lines, and passed his work to Shaw. After a short time, Shaw announced, 'Look here, I've written half the first act of that comedy, and I've used up all your plot. Now I want some more to go on with.' One can imagine Archer's fury. The play was abandoned.

In response to Grein's request, Shaw recovered the fragments of the play he had written, added a third act and gave his work a mock-Biblical title, *Widowers' Houses*. It was a polemical attack on what he called 'slum landlordism', which he considered to be the pattern of the capitalist system as he knew it. A modest production at the Royalty Theatre in 1892 was received in the customary uproar, with praise or blame bestowed according to the political persuasion of the spectator. Upon the call for 'Author!', Shaw, nothing loath, promptly delivered a lecture from the stage on the subject of socialism. But the event was of greater consequence than the virtues and limitations of one performance, or even of the play itself. It marked the discovery by the Society of a major playwright, and showed a keen new writer what a powerful platform the theatre could provide at the command of someone who had something to say, especially if he was a little messianic. Shaw rose next morning to find himself infamous overnight, which rather appealed to his nature, and, for a new playwright, was certainly better than nothing at all.

Nobody would take on Shaw's next play, his unattractive, if witty, treatment of unhappy marriage, sexual manners and one Leonard Charteris, a selfish and unscrupulous Don Juan. This was *The Philanderer* (1893), a comedy in which Shaw threw together Ibsenites and non-Ibsenites as a way of talking about the new social freedom. However, Shaw had already written another that same year, and this play was to do for Shaw what *A Doll's House* had done for Ibsen.

Mrs Warren's Profession is Shaw's moral study of the economics of prostitution, no less, and even Grein resisted it. The play begins perversely and deceptively on a lovely summer afternoon in a cottage garden, with a pretty girl lying in a hammock. Moreover, prostitution and what became known as the white slave trade are never mentioned in the play; its subject lies as a hidden tension behind its witty comedy. The truth is that Mrs Warren is a procuress whose international chain of brothels has paid for her daughter Vivie's expensive education at Cambridge, and we discover this appalling fact along with Vivie herself. Mrs Warren's partner in crime tells the girl, 'Do you remember your scholarship at Cambridge? Well, that was founded by my brother. He gets his 22% out of a factory with 600 girls in it, and not one of them getting wages enough to live on. How d'ye suppose they manage when they have no family to fall back on? Ask your mother.' Vivie is made to feel an accomplice in the crime of seizing an education.

But Shaw was not writing a sentimental melodrama, and Mrs Warren is not presented as a villainess. Instead, he tricks us, as he at first tricks Vivie, into accepting Mrs Warren's justification for her actions: 'What is any respectable girl brought up to do but to catch some rich man's fancy and get the benefit of his money by marrying him? — as if a marriage ceremony could make any difference in the right or wrong of the thing!' So Vivie has been sent to college to take a brilliant degree in mathematics, and then to study actuarial law — she is to make money as men do, and never have to prostitute herself. Vivie is among the first of the Shavian 'new

9. Shaw, *Mrs Warren's Profession*, 1902. First production, Act II, with Fanny Brough and Madge McIntosh.

women', the 'unwomanly' women, and she enjoys a cigar, a glass of whisky and a good detective story after work. In the last scene she becomes an adult, when, with a touch of pathos, she spurns her mother and her good as well as her bad intentions. Vivie is still young, and she will work out the future for herself on sounder principles. Even then, Mrs Warren is still not the villain. But, we may ask, if Shaw is not attacking her, and if he is not defending her, who then is the villain of the piece? Says Shaw, society is, for we must all share the complicity in a social crime.

Mrs Warren's Profession has all the characteristic Shavian shocks, but it hardly helped his image as a playwright. He afterwards stated, 'I could not have done anything more injurious to my prospects at the outset of my career.' The Lord Chamberlain would not entertain the play, and it did not get on the stage for eight years, when in 1902 it at last evaded the censorship with two private performances done by the Stage Society. Grein's comments on this production convey some idea of the unease felt by its audience:

> It was an exceedingly uncomfortable afternoon, for there was a majority of women to listen to that which could only be understood by a minority of men... And, sure as I feel that most of the women, and a good many of the men ... did not at first know, and finally merely guessed, what was the women's trade, I cannot withhold the opinion that the representation was unnecessary and painful... Now [Shaw] has merely philandered around a dangerous subject; he has treated it half in earnest, half in that peculiar jesting manner which is all his own. He has given free reins to his brain and silenced his heart.

As for Archer, good friend that he was, he had found *Widowers' Houses* cynical, and now found *Mrs Warren* wholly unacceptable: 'What is fundamentally intolerable in the play is its almost all-pervading flippancy of tone.' Behind these judgments on Shaw's jesting manner and flippant tone lie hints of what was to become his peculiar brand of realism.

Another 'morbidly curious audience' of New Yorkers packed the Garrick Theatre in 1905 for Arnold Daly's production of *Mrs*

Warren's Profession (with Daly himself playing Frank). It had opened
in New Haven and had been almost well received before the police
closed in. Now its notoriety preceded it. *The American* called the
play 'illuminated gangrene', and the *New York Herald* found the
play, as the London press had done, 'morally rotten', and considered
that 'the limit of stage indecency has been reached' (31 October).
This notice was full of staccato cries:

> It defends immorality.
> It glorifies debauchery.
> It besmirches the sacredness of a
> clergyman's calling, etc., etc.,

but it did quote Daly's speech before the curtain:

> This play is not presented as an entertainment, but as a
> dramatic sermon and an exposé of a social condition and
> an evil which our purists attempt to ignore.

In spite of this, the outcry in the press compelled the police to arrest
Daly and his whole company, and he was morally lynched for
months before the courts vindicated him. Characteristically, Shaw
asserted that it was a triumph to send 'a pallid crowd of critics into
the street shrieking that the pillars of society are cracking and the
ruin of the State is at hand'. But Shaw's early plays made better
progress in America than in Britain, perhaps because the apparently
pro-revolutionary play *The Devil's Disciple* had had a first production
in Albany in 1897. In Britain, on the other hand, the ban on *Mrs
Warren* was not lifted until 1925, but by that time the public had
grown more used to Shaw and his sensations.

As dramatic critic to *The Saturday Review* from 1895 to 1898,
Shaw had repeatedly condemned the pedestrian thinking of the
romantic drama and the mechanics of the well-made play. In his
own account of why he had abandoned Archer's plot scenario for
Widowers' Houses, he explained how his method of writing a play
was to tell 'the story', something which grew out of the imagination;
it was not 'a manufactured article constructed by an artisan according to plans and specifications'. We should remember that Shaw was
an admirer of Shelley as well as of Ibsen. When the critics argued
that his plays, being didactic in intention, could not be works of art,

he proudly proclaimed himself to be a didactic playwright indeed, and insisted that *Widowers' Houses* was 'a propagandist play – a didactic play – a play with a purpose ... deliberately intended to induce people to vote on the Progressive side at the next County Council election in London'. In sum, Shaw believed that all great drama must teach, and his name was thereafter inseparably associated with the idea of the thesis play.

As a writer of problem plays, Shaw also believed that he was following in Ibsen's footsteps, and Shaw's enthusiasm for Ibsen was never so well demonstrated as in *The Quintessence of Ibsenism* (1891). It is a commonplace of criticism that this lively book tells us more about the younger Shaw than about Ibsen: the Irishman seems blind to larger questions of the human spirit which increasingly concerned the poet in Ibsen. Shaw actually said the work was 'simply an exposition of Ibsen', and not until 1913 were chapters added on the last four plays beginning with *The Master Builder*, Ibsen's most symbolic plays. It is worth remembering that *The Quintessence of Ibsenism* started life as a lecture to the Fabian Society on the general theme of Socialism in Contemporary Literature, which in part explains its provocative tone.

Shaw thought of Ibsen as a great teacher and critic of society, intent upon attacking what Shaw considered to be our slavery to ideals and idealism. The gospel according to Shaw required that we be ready to criticize our ideals, which was a form of salutary self-criticism. An idealist shirks the truth, whereas a realist faces it. He knew that realists and pioneers must inevitably trample on idealists, inevitably profane what was sacred. It followed that in Shaw's eyes, a Torvald who followed the ideal in the role of the man who was a villain, and that a leading lady who rejected the ideal of womanliness was bound to seem an unwomanly woman. The basis of an Ibsen play was that human behaviour should justify itself by its effect on life, and not by conforming to some ideal: 'The golden rule is that there are no golden rules.'

In practice this meant that a play would have the power to hold the stage if it raised problems of personal importance to an audience; it made 'a moralist and a debater' of the problem play dramatist. When Nora of *A Doll's House* said at the emotional crisis of the play, 'We must sit down and talk about what has happened', it was as if she had founded a new style of performance, said Shaw. But why wait for the end of a play for the discussion, when the audience was tired? Why should not the discussion 'interpenetrate the action'? And if there were no moral right or wrong in formal debate, why should there be heroes and villains in a play? So in *The Quintessence of Ibsenism* Shaw arrived at his first theory of the new drama, although taking the name of Ibsen a little in vain. For the old tricks of playwriting,

> Ibsen substituted a terrible art of sharpshooting at the audience, trapping them, fencing with them, aiming always at the sorest spot in their consciences. Never mislead an audience, was an old rule. But the new school will trick the spectator into forming a meanly false judgment, and then convict him of it in the next act, often to his grievous mortification... In the theatre of Ibsen we are not flattered spectators killing an idle hour with an ingenious and amusing entertainment: we are 'guilty creatures sitting at a play'; and the technique of pastime is no more applicable than at a murder trial (pp. 145–6).

In *The New Review* of November 1891, Archer was quick to point out that Shaw had got it all wrong, and that Ibsen was no social prophet: 'Ibsen had no gospel whatever, in the sense of a systematic body of knowledge.' It is true that Shaw's simple pattern of 'realists' and 'idealists' destroys the subtlety of Ibsen's characterization, but the new dramatic philosophy exactly described Shaw's own kind of evangelism, and supplied the clue to his early craft as a playwright.

As Shaw pursued his theory, so he also persistently attacked traditional Victorian acting. He called Irving's performances, for example, ones of 'hackneyed stage tricks'. He saw the need for a new school of acting, which merely required that actors shake off their sentimental stock roles. A selfish idealist was not necessarily a villain, nor an unselfish realist a hero; nor was a satirical portrait automatically the job for a comic actor. Helmer was not a hypocritical Joseph Surface, nor Gregers Werle of *The Wild Duck* a clownish George Washington, devotee of truth. An Ibsen character could not be played like a theatrical convention, since it was its very ambiguity that gave it life on the stage. The new actor must be so 'plastic' that he could assume whatever shape the individual character needed. And Shaw named Janet Achurch (who had played Nora), Florence Farr (who had played Rebecca West in *Rosmersholm*) and the Americans Elizabeth Robins and Marion Lea (respectively Hedda and Thea in *Hedda Gabler*) as actresses happily too new to have been trapped into stereotyped performances. Nevertheless, Shaw also recognized that, as a pioneer of stagecraft, Ibsen would meet a great deal of opposition from actors, managers and critics when it became clear that a new acting style was needed to match the new realism. In the event, it was not Shaw but his friend Harley Granville-Barker who addressed himself, in both criticism and practice, to the problems of making the transition on the English stage from one style of acting to another, and to achieving the change from a theatre where the actor dominated to one where the dramatist presided.

It is a nice irony of Shavian dramatic theory, therefore, that what is more didactic can be more real. In his 'Author's Apology' in the Preface to *Mrs Warren's Profession*, he reiterated his belief that 'fine art is the subtlest, the most seductive, the most effective instrument of moral propaganda in the world'. He was particularly outraged by the censorship imposed upon the play, with the damning implication that it could corrupt its audiences. 'I am the last man to deny', he said, 'that if the net effect of performing *Mrs Warren's Profession* were an increase in the number of persons entering that profession or employing it, its performance might well be made an indictable offence.' Instead of the play of romantic sentiment, he had offered the problem play of 'remorseless logic' with an iron framework of fact'. To he arrived at the conclusion that drama was 'no mere setting up of the camera to nature: it is the presentation in parable of the conflict between Man's will and his environment'. His characters were therefore more like human beings than the creatures who conformed to romantic convention. Would any girl treat her mother as Vivie Warren does? asked Shaw. Not in the romantic drama: only in real life.

Shaw knew the limitations of the problem play, however. In a contribution to *The Humanitarian* for May 1895, entitled, 'Should social questions be freely dealt with in the drama?', he argued that if a play dealt with the fundamental processes of life, it would help it survive on the stage: 'A drama with a social question for the motive cannot outlive the solution of that question.' When the struggle is between man and a purely legal institution, 'nothing can prolong its life beyond that of the institution'. The great writers assimilated everything, including social and political questions, but in the end their theme was humanity as a whole, as in *Hamlet*, *Faust* and *Peer Gynt*. Nevertheless, transitory questions can have magnitude, and so Shaw reached another seemingly contradictory conclusion: '*A Doll's House* will be as flat as ditchwater when *A Midsummer Night's Dream* will still be as fresh as paint, but it will have done more work in the world.'

Shaw modified this view of the problem play a few years later. He continued to assert that merely to amuse an audience was no work for a great artist, but in his preface to *Three Plays by Brieux* in 1911, he added that the artist had 'to interpret life', and went on to explain this pious phrase. The daily events and incidents of life were meaningless to us until they were arranged in significant relationships. The great artist thus changed us 'from bewildered spectators of a monstrous confusion to men intelligently conscious of the world and its destinies'.

We have now heard most of the individual notes of Shavian realism. He never felt the need to present a slice of life on the stage; to do this was a 'mere setting up of the camera to nature'. He wrote to drive home a point. Truth to life, however, was his first and last object as a writer, and therefore a play like *Widowers' Houses* would never, he felt, be 'a beautiful or lovable work':

> It is saturated with the vulgarity of the life it represents:
> the people do not speak nobly, live gracefully, or sincerely
> face their own position: the author is not giving expression
> in pleasant fancies to the underlying beauty and romance of
> happy life, but dragging up to the smooth surface of 'res-
> pectability' a handful of the slime and foulness of its
> polluted bed, and playing off your laughter at the scandal of
> the exposure against your shudder at its blackness.

So he wrote in his Preface to the play. In time, however, Shaw's bad experience with the censorship and the mixed reception of his plays brought him round to the view that he must practice to deceive. He learned to disarm his critics with their laughter, adopt the method of the clown and the absurdist, and eventually use the form and conventions of the popular drama itself in order to lower their defences. The flippancy present in all his work came increasingly to the fore,

10. Shaw, *Arms and the Man*, Avenue Theatre, London, 1894. Act I, with Alma Murray and Yorke Stephens.

and he called his next group of plays 'plays pleasant', in the belief that most people believe what they see in print. These next plays were *Arms and the Man* (1894), *Candida* (1895) and *You Never Can Tell* (1899) — a scintillating trio and among the best of Shaw's comedies.

Arms and the Man coated the pill with sugar in abundance, and it is included here as a transitional play, a compromise with the severities of the 'plays unpleasant', in that it uses the burlesque form (in spite of Shaw's disclaimers) to disguise its anti-war theme. Unlike the earlier plays, its composition was quickly followed by a production at the Avenue Theatre in London. It was warmly applauded and ran for fifty nights. At the same time, it threw Shaw's critics into some confusion. In the play the comic little world of Bulgaria is shown trying to keep pace with western civilization and the skills of war, and so it comically embodies all the ideals and illusions of the age. Into the play comes a Swiss officer, Bluntschli, a veteran professional soldier and a highly sophisticated realist intent upon shattering the audience's beliefs about the army. Soldiering was an inglorious business. Bluntschli was promptly condemned as a coward, for it was inconceivable that there could be any limit to a soldier's courage in the face of the enemy, or that he might prefer to live rather than die a glorious death. This Swiss officer shies like a frightened horse when a girl snatches a box of chocolates from him, and seems to confirm the verdict of cowardice; but this was simply Shaw's light-hearted way of suggesting how a soldier feels after three days under fire. Bluntschli is set in sharp contrast with Sergius, the Bulgarian cavalry captain who charges the enemy like a raw recruit, or, as Shaw says in his amusing defence of the play, 'A Dramatic Realist to His Critics' in *The New Review* for July 1894, like a stage hero who finds in death 'the supreme consolation of being able to get up and go home when the curtain falls'. Bluntschli carries chocolate into battle instead of cartridges, knowing that survival depends upon food as much as on weapons, and the critics therefore mistook him for 'a poltroon who prefers chocolates to fighting'. Only A. B. Walkley in *The Speaker* of 28 April saw that this Swiss soldier was being frankly presented as an unromantic, but was a real man nonetheless.

The critics had little to measure this kind of play by, and the consensus was that it was a form of 'Gilbertian extravaganza'. In *The*

World, Archer found it very funny, and 'not a serious comedy', even if Shaw did dwell 'on the seamy side to the exclusion of all else'; but Archer added encouragingly, 'I begin positively to believe that he may one day write a serious and even an artistic play.' *The Star* thought the play 'enormously amusing, if slightly perplexing. . . One does not always see what [Shaw] is driving at', a troubling sentiment which was echoed in the *Tribune* when the play opened in New York the same year: William Winter thought the play enjoyable 'if he stopped looking for a meaning in it'. Again, only Walkley found there to be a serious core to it: 'In the form of a droll, fantastic farce, it presents us with a criticism of conduct, a theory of life.'

Arms and the Man was also made to the formula for the well-made play, and its comparative success proved one thing to its author, that, like Molière, a playwright could teach a better lesson in the theatre by exploiting the traditional methods *of* the theatre, a chief of which is comedy. Luckily, Shaw was a born jester.

Shaw's career as a playwright was more immediately helped when a second Stage Society, based on the same principles as Grein's, sprang to life in London in 1899 under an outstanding Council of Management which included J. M. Barrie, Granville-Barker, St John Hankin and Shaw himself. The Stage Society existed, it declared, 'to promote and encourage Dramatic Art' and 'to serve as an Experimental Theatre'. It opened with Shaw's *You Never Can Tell*, and proved to be his life-line, for it produced *Captain Brassbound's Conversion* (1900), the first *Candida* in 1902, the *Mrs Warren's Profession* of 1902 and *Man and Superman* (1905). And in 1904, Shaw was helped again by the new repertory experiment at the Court Theatre, Sloane Square, under the management of Vedrenne and Granville-Barker, an outstanding experiment which was to last for three years.

At the Court, three-quarters of the productions were of Shaw's plays, earning it the popular name of 'The Shaw Repertory Theatre'. The company, which included young actors of the calibre of Lewis Casson, built a new public for Shaw, whose strengths as a playwright became increasingly visible. In 1907, the company moved to the Savoy Theatre to continue its policy, but after one season it unfortunately failed as a commercial enterprise. During this time, Shaw owed a great deal to the quality of Barker's acting and directing, although Barker's greater contribution was to develop a contemporary, and distinctly English, style of underplaying for the realistic drama. He favoured what he called the more 'implicit' playwriting of Ibsen and Chekhov, and did not much relish Shaw's more old-fashioned, 'explicit' or operatic style. It is not surprising to learn that Shaw on occasion conducted his own rehearsals, when he took enormous pleasure in reading the play aloud to the actors, and suggesting the rhetorical manner he wanted by jumping on to the stage himself and playing all the parts. By the time that the original impulse of the independent theatre movement had passed, Shaw was moving fast along tracks of his own.

Barker believed that Shaw had discovered his form and style in Italian opera, and it is true that Shaw was fond of pointing out that music had more sensory enchantment than the drama. *Romeo and Juliet*, for example, was 'dry, tedious and rhetorical' beside *Tristan und Isolde*, and Shaw argued that the only drama without music which could compete with opera was the 'drama of thought'. It is certainly hard to recognize the early realism of Ibsen and Strindberg in the mature Shavian plays. Rather, there is a clear line of English comedy to be traced through the wit and repartee of *Much Ado About Nothing, The Man of Mode, The School for Scandal* and *Candida*, and an even clearer line of female characterization to be followed from Rosalind, Margery Pinchwife and Kate Hardcastle to Ann Whitefield of *Man and Superman*. In a final analysis, the distinctive quality of *Candida* and *Man and Superman* would owe little to naturalism, and much to a keen sense of a comic stage traditional to English drama, one in which social and sexual conventions are kept well in proportion by a gentle teasing, and even the 'new woman' turns out to be of quite ancient lineage. Mixing a little of W. S. Gilbert and his satirical burlesque with Oscar Wilde's iconoclastic wit, and adding his own operatic flourishes, Shaw brought a sharper purpose to his comedy than either of these. Yet they are more his kin than the sober Scandinavians.

Shaw's role in the history of English drama was to elevate the serious theatre in London to a status it had not known for over a century, even if no one could walk in his giant footsteps. All the same, it was never certain that he was truly dealing in realism and not some special brand of Shavian practical joke which required all participants to see that the truth always has two sides, if not more.

---

10 *Realism in Russia: Nemirovich-Danchenko, Stanislavsky and the Moscow Art Theatre*

The Seagull (1898), *The Lower Depths* (1902)

It is ironic that the best answers to the practical challenges of the new realism — how the actor should match his art to the new dialogue, and how the writer should adapt his writing to the new techniques of the stage — did not come from Copenhagen or Paris or Berlin. It came from a city generally considered to be on the fringes of western theatre. Upon the creation of the Moscow Art Theatre by two giants of the modern stage, Nemirovich-Danchenko and Konstantin Stanislavsky, Moscow became the new centre of the naturalistic movement, and in the years that followed it was the fountainhead of the theory and method which nourished realistic acting and production everywhere. Where other companies succeeded only in imitating the surface of real life, the MAT realized its psychological depth.

Vladimir Ivanovich Nemirovich-Danchenko (1858–1943) was a respected playwright and novelist in his own right, and it was a literary and critical sensitivity which enabled him to recognize the quality of a new play. He had also been a director and manager of the Moscow Imperial Dramatic Theatre, and it was his administrative ability which enabled the MAT to stay alive during the artistically demanding years of its beginning, and into the revolutionary years of the new Soviet state. These talents also combined to prepare him for the major theatrical upheaval which he and Stanislavsky were to cause. Danchenko was responsible for the planning of the world's leading repertory theatre, one which set such standards in professional discipline that it became the envy of every director.

Danchenko is known outside Russia only by his autobiography *My Life in the Russian Theatre*; inside Russia he was known as a great director and teacher of acting. He worked to create natural speech and behaviour in the actor, and what he called the actor's 'sincerity of experience'. Like Stanislavsky, he expected the actor to 'live' his part rather than merely present it, to feel and not merely 'act' an emotion, and on this basis Danchenko formulated a 'law of inner justification'. Like Stanislavsky again, he believed in the presence of a single will or spirit behind a production, that of the *régisseur*, whose 'intuition' should 'infect' everyone connected with the performance. Only then would the play assume a proper unity of style and atmosphere.

Konstantin Sergeyevich Stanislavsky (1863–1938) was born into a wealthy and influential family with artistic and theatrical leanings. Signs of his unusual dedication as an actor and director appeared early, when at twenty-four he urged his amateur cast to practise Japanese manners in preparation for a production of *The Mikado* of Gilbert and Sullivan; he even had the women tie their legs above the knee to remind them to walk with tiny steps. There was more than a touch of misplaced ingenuity in taking a burlesque comic opera so seriously. For ten years after its founding in 1888, he acted with the Society of Art and Literature, a group of enthusiastic amateurs, and during this time was inspired by the standards of realistic production he saw in the work of Chronegk and the Meiningen company. These standards Stanislavsky applied in Chronegk's own despotic way to productions of *Othello*, Hauptmann's *Hannele* and Tolstoy's *The Fruits of Enlightenment*, which owed to Stanislavsky its first production.

After this initiation, Stanislavsky was ready to form a permanent company, so that, as his work showed less of the trappings of external realism and more of the inner qualities of psychological honesty, the MAT had its beginnings in a more evolutionary than revolutionary way. In 1897, the famous meeting between Stanislavsky and Danchenko took place in a restaurant at the Slavyansky Bazaar in Moscow, where they found they had enough in common to talk for eighteen hours. At the end of that marathon, they had together drawn up the rules for a new kind of theatre. They determined to discard what was bad in the past, indeed everything that was characteristic of Moscow's leading commercial theatre, the Maly. Out would go the cheap repertoire of French and German farces, the star system that denied the possibility of ensemble work, and the declamatory manner of acting with all its stale theatrical tricks and habits. All of this had, of course, been heard before in Paris and Berlin, but never before was so stringent a set of rules drawn up for the members of a company. Any self-indulgence on the part of an actor was to be regarded as a crime, and any temperamental behaviour, lateness or laziness was to be forbidden: 'One must love art, and not oneself in art'. Actors were to be chosen for their devotion to work: 'There are no small parts; there are only small actors'. Thus did Stanislavsky's epigrams come into circulation. Rehearsals were to last as long as twelve hours a day, and would be conducted in an atmosphere of reverence for the drama. Dedication like this was good and necessary, provided it did not become bigotry.

The press at first found the new company something of a joke. Since it rehearsed in a barn some way out of Moscow, it was suggested, for example, that crickets had been brought in to add realism to the stagecraft. As it turned out, this was not far wrong, but in any case it was all good publicity. With the ardent support of his designer Victor A. Simov, Stanislavsky aimed at an historical authenticity on the stage never known before — not Charles Kean with his antiquarian Shakespeare, nor the Meiningens with all their visual detail of realistic illusion.

The first production of the Moscow Art Theatre in 1898 was a fair test of the new ideals: it was of Alexey Tolstoy's rambling historical piece, *Tsar Fyodor*. This play was given no less than seventy-four rehearsals, including five dress rehearsals. It became a sixteenth-century research project of the first magnitude, with the whole company going off on numerous field trips to museums, monasteries, palaces, bazaars and fairs, in order to recreate on the stage an authentic reproduction of life in old Russia, with its meals and manners, its clothing and jewelry, the correct weapons and furniture, and all the rest. The audience was treated to replicas of rooms in the Kremlin, the Cathedral and a bridge over the River Yaouza with barges passing beneath. For one device, the palace ceilings and doors were lowered to make the Boyars seem taller on

Russ

finar
Chek
fect
conv
Thea
been
dialc
impe
type
inad
com
audi
awk
Chel
anot
The
capt
was
tion
its a
to p

twe
deta
a sc
kinc
Star
evei
the
moc
test
ing
abs(
play
of i
app
fied
the

their ritualistic entrance. The audience was dazzled, so much so that it was hardly aware of the natural speech, realistic acting and team-work achieved by Ivan Moskvin and Olga Knipper as the Tsar and Tsarine, and by Vishnevsky as their strong minister Boris Godunov, The production established the new theatre overnight, and period plays in the realistic manner became a common feature of the repertoire for more than twenty-five years —indeed, they remain one of the strengths of modern Russian production on stage and screen generally.

It is of some interest that when the MAT brought *Tsar Fyodor* to New York in 1923, a generation later, certain doubts were ex-pressed. The authenticity of the ensemble acting, costume and décor impressed everyone; but Stark Young, that most perceptive of theatre critics, nevertheless raised an objection which suggested that only certain features of the new style might survive. He declared that he had 'no interest in poetry taken as prose, and almost no interest in history taken ... as contemporaneous human life'. He missed 'the magic of distance and scope, the conscious arrangement, the artifice and logic, that would create in my mind the idea'. And he deplored the loss of 'great style', which should remain in the mind 'like music, like great poetry, great abstractions'. For Stark Young, it seems, the realism of the MAT had already reached a limit.

If one wonders at the MAT's *Othello*, which involved the whole company in a research expedition to Cyprus, or at the pedantry of importing Norwegian furniture for *Hedda Gabler* and *The Enemy of the People*, or at the slavish requirement that the actors live in togas for several days before the opening of *Julius Caesar*, it was this quality of careful truth to life which also encouraged a new degree of psychology in the playing. The MAT's ability to embrace the sub-tleties of *contemporary* realism in all its aspects marked its dif-ference from the Meiningen company. Without a complete com-mitment to an ideal of realism, the early successes of Chekhov's *The Seagull* in the production of 1898, *Uncle Vanya* (1899) and *The Lower Depths* (1902) by Maxim Gorky (1868–1936) would not have been possible. *The Lower Depths* was in fact the direct result of Gorky's seeing the kind of work the company could achieve with Chekhov. To these plays should be added Tolstoy's fierce indictment of human nature in his censored peasant play *The Power of Darkness*, which

received
piece, St₂
from Tu
imagine
   Th

At this distance, we are in a position to make a balanced judgment. Set design still belonged to the age of the scene painter, and Simov's work would have pleased us less today. In his memoirs, he reported that the painting of the lake for act I was too photo-graphic for Chekhov's liking, whose work in the last analysis is more impressionistic. Chekhov's dry comment on Simov's lake was, 'Well, it is wet', and one suspects that a hint of moonlight on water would have sufficed. Stanislavsky's request for a chill in the air during the last act, in order to convey the emptiness of the family's life, was better met by Simov, who hit upon the idea of placing the furniture on the stage in some disorder, so that its appearance suggested the indifference of those assumed to live with it.

Stanislavsky's 'score' for the play was recorded carefully in a notebook, and this has been conveniently edited by S. D. Balukhaty and translated by David Magarshack with the title *The Seagull Produced by Stanislavsky*. The concern for detail is apparent through-out, but the question remains, What kind of detail? Stanislavsky was not past using conventional ways of inducing emotion. At the end of the play, for example, Nina makes a last appearance to show

12. Chekhov, *The Seagull*, Moscow Art Theatre, 1898. Production by Stanislavsky. Act I, set by V.A. Simov.

11.
St

finances of the company, but sent it on a greater quest: to find life in Chekhov's delicate nuances of atmosphere and mood, and to perfect an acting technique which would render his characters totally convincing. The play had failed miserably at the Alexandrinsky Theatre in St Petersburg in 1896, precisely because its actors had been unable to meet its psychological demands. The colloquial dialogue deceived them and the outlines of the characters seemed imperceptible. Even Vera Kommissarzhevskaya played Nina as the type of an abused maiden. Trained by the old professional rules and inadequately prepared, the players trusted that inspiration would come on the night. It did not, and the result was a disaster. The audience found Treplev's attempt at suicide a great joke, and the awkward symbolism of the property seagull quite ridiculous. Chekhov was crushed, and left the theatre swearing never to write another play. Danchenko, however, perceived the fresh qualities in *The Seagull*; it was written, he thought, in 'semitones' designed to capture a fragile mood of unhappiness. He also recognized that it was just the kind of play the new company needed to give it direction. Stanislavsky confessed that he had not understood 'its essence, its aroma, its beauty' at the time, but he agreed to let Danchenko try to persuade Chekhov to let them have the play.

With characteristic earnestness, Stanislavsky gave *The Seagull* twenty-six rehearsals. The time was devoted to perfecting every detail of speech and gesture in order to capture the elusive tone of a scene, and Chekhov's genius for observed detail rewarded this kind of approach as few dramatists could have done. Moreover, Stanislavsky's respect for his author grew as he discovered how well every touch of character and action contributed to the whole, and by the first night, every member of the company was aware that a new mode of performance, a new kind of play, was to suffer its crucial test. The silence of the audience during the first act was nerve-wracking for the cast, but it was soon apparent that this indicated its total absorption. The audience had been caught up in the mesh of the play's details, and was responding to Stanislavsky's orchestration of its rhythms. At the final curtain the house broke into a roar of applause, and all the MAT's meticulous preparation seemed justified. *The Seagull* truly inaugurated a new era in Russian theatre, and the exultant company appropriately adopted a seagull as its emblem.

At this distance, we are in a position to make a balanced judgment. Set design still belonged to the age of the scene painter, and Simov's work would have pleased us less today. In his memoirs, he reported that the painting of the lake for act I was too photographic for Chekhov's liking, whose work in the last analysis is more impressionistic. Chekhov's dry comment on Simov's lake was, 'Well, it is wet', and one suspects that a hint of moonlight on water would have sufficed. Stanislavsky's request for a chill in the air during the last act, in order to convey the emptiness of the family's life, was better met by Simov, who hit upon the idea of placing the furniture on the stage in some disorder, so that its appearance suggested the indifference of those assumed to live with it.

Stanislavsky's 'score' for the play was recorded carefully in a notebook, and this has been conveniently edited by S. D. Balukhaty and translated by David Magarshack with the title *The Seagull Produced by Stanislavsky*. The concern for detail is apparent throughout, but the question remains, What kind of detail? Stanislavsky was not past using conventional ways of inducing emotion. At the end of the play, for example, Nina makes a last appearance to show

12. Chekhov, *The Seagull*, Moscow Art Theatre, 1898. Production by Stanislavsky. Act I, set by V.A. Simov.

how time has changed her into a more mature person, and Stanislavsky's pauses accordingly drew out the suspense — he created
and groped his way through nineteen such pauses in this act alone.
The repeated counterpoint of laughter in the next room, particularly
from the apparent 'seducer' Trigorin, squeezed out the last drop of
pathos. Stanislavsky knew he was using old stage trickery, and was
not ashamed to say so: his jotting on the subject of this laughter is,
'It never misses with an audience', and we should know that Chekhov himself had first suggested it. However, such signs of Chekhov's
weakness for the melodramatic in this scene, at this stage in his
career as a playwright, might have been all the more reason why his
director should have corrected the tendency.

Stanislavsky's Nina leaned towards the stereotype of the for-
saken girl, although the author had written lines that belonged to a
wiser, more decisive Nina, who, by choosing to leave Treplev, was
telling him to grow up. More than this, Stanislavsky had the scene
played against an obtrusive storm outside the house, and this was
arranged to smash a pane of glass at the crisis. The tolling of a
church bell afar off added to the tempestuous atmosphere, and
Treplev even dropped a glass of water from lifeless fingers upon
Nina's departure. In a letter to his friend Suvorin, Chekhov said
that he had ended the play *pianissimo*, 'contrary to all the rules of
dramatic art', but this infringement was evidently corrected by his
director. It therefore remains in doubt who earned the roar of
applause at the curtain of the first production of *The Seagull*, Chekhov
or Stanislavsky.

The Lower Depths is not as demanding a play as *The Seagull*,
but Gorky had written it in what he took to be a Chekhovian
manner. In fact it was far more politically coloured than anything
Moscow had seen on the stage before, and its portrait of human
degradation in a doss-house in a provincial town on the Volga was
a strong comment on social conditions in Tsarist Russia. Replete
with grim realistic details of thievery, alcoholism, prostitution and
violence, the play lent itself fully to the new methods, and the cast
promptly went off to inspect some actual institutions of lower life in
Moscow's notorious Khitrov Market. In performance, the actors
wore real rags, so that some spectators feared they might catch
lice from being too near the stage. But Gorky was not Chekhov, and

the characters of *The Lower Depths* are more strident, less understated, than those of his friend. While remaining plotless and impressionistic in its realism, the play reverts to the pattern of the
French thesis-play, driven by the need to preach. To avoid the
theatricality of a propaganda piece, Stanislavsky worked for
simplicity and sincerity in the speaking, and sought finally, as he
said in *My Life in Art*, 'to enter into the springs of Gorky himself'
(translated J. J. Robbins).

The production was an overwhelming success in Russia, but
again an unusual objection was heard from Stark Young when he
saw it in New York in 1923. He praised the scenes of 'pure theatre',
like the scene of Luka the pilgrim when he ministers to the dying
woman: this was 'poetic realism'. But, he added, 'character after
character stood out to the eye, heavily accented, without a blur'.
Stanislavsky himself, who played Satine the card-sharper, was the
worst, he said, since his whole costume and appearance was of
shreds and patches: 'everything insufferably scored – as his
speeches, for all their great intelligence, were scored – like the work
of a brilliant amateur'. We can sense this from the photographs of
the time, with every character playing the part for all he is worth.

Many have commented with amusement on Stanislavsky's
excesses in pursuit of surface realism, especially the sound effects
he dearly loved: the crickets and frogs, the birds and dogs in *The
Seagull*, *Uncle Vanya*'s creaking swing, the insistent fire-alarms and
fire-engines (not to mention the famous sound of a Stanislavsky
mouse) in *Three Sisters*, and mosquitoes, frogs and corncrakes in
The Cherry Orchard, together with a train passing in the distance, had
Chekhov allowed it.

As both actor and director, Stanislavsky was also inclined to
romanticize Chekhov's intentionally dry characters, so that his
Trigorin was more of an elderly roué, his Astrov more of a passionate lover, his Vershinin too pathetic. Stanislavsky's published
notebooks on *The Seagull*, *The Lower Depths* and *Othello* reveal how
his imagination as a director frequently led him right away from his
author's play. These notebooks are highly detailed (act I of *The Lower
Depths* includes thirty-nine diagrams alone), and were clearly
composed in the study, with only what Stanislavsky called his
'inner eye and ear' on the stage. They suggest the approach of an

enthusiastic director likely to impose his own ideas at the expense of the very actors who must discover their own answers. Stanislavsky later perceived his error as he began to work towards a greater psychological realism of character, and found it necessary for director and actor to 'grow together' in their work on a play.

None of these criticisms, however, should belittle Stanislavsky's unique achievement in uncovering the psychological attributes required of an actor to bring a literary creature to life on the stage. Over the years, Stanislavsky taught acting in the various studios of the MAT, and, prolific note-keeper and diarist that he was, constantly analysed everything he did. Thanks to this, he left us with a full account of how an actor might school himself to find a character's motives in his own mind. Indeed, Stanislavsky, and what he called his 'System', or what became known in America as 'The Method', have dominated schools of acting in this century. So far three books in English have collected his teachings: *An Actor Prepares* (1936), *Building a Character* (1949) and *Creating a Role* (1961).

The Stanislavsky System was intended to be as natural and organic, he said, as the growth of a tree, since it was based essentially on intuition and not on science or logic. Unhappily, a wealth of technical jargon associated with the System has grown up, and in the following outline of Stanislavsky's ideas, the terms that are current have been italicized for quick recognition.

1. The *super-objective* or *ruling idea* of a play often, though not necessarily, interprets the main direction of the plot: thus, Hamlet wishes to cleanse the world of evil, or, the three sisters wish to return to Moscow. All other dramatic elements subserve the super-objective which should help the actor find the *perspective of his role*, in order that he may relate his work to the whole. *Subtext* was a notion devised chiefly for the reform of nineteenth-century acting, after it was considered inadequate for a true performance merely to memorize the lines set down; the subtext, or *inner life*, of a part would supply the actor with clues to his hidden motives in the play.

2. Working from the 'facts' of the play, an actor's creativeness springs from his belief in the truth of the life on the stage in its *given circumstances*, the *magic if* behind the life to be created (*If* you were in love with Juliet, what would you do?). The actor seeks the feeling

of *inner truth*, or *inner logic*, in his part, the *logic of the emotions*, and he begins to assume a character's psychological make-up by studying his *pre-text*, or what is suggested about his imaginary life before the curtain rises. The given circumstances at the beginning of *Hamlet* might be that the Prince had just returned from his father's grave-side, and at the beginning of *The Seagull* that Nina had just been quarrelling with her father.

3. With some sense of his part's inner truth, an actor can *motivate* all the details of his speech, gesture and movement on the stage. To facilitate this, he should divide the part into several minor *objectives* or *fragments*, which will then grow from one another when played in sequence. Imaginative exercises, loosely related to the play itself, can help place the actor in his *imaginary circle*, and help him recreate a living character by a personal effort of the will and memory. This *psycho-technique* compels him to evoke the appropriate *memory of emotions*, and to transfer to the stage his personal exper-ience, his *inner images* from the past. This process is 'the conscious stimulation of the unconscious'. Thus, as an exercise, an actress might improvise a scene from Mme Ranevsky's life in Paris before she returned to the cherry orchard by recalling a party of her own that she did not fully enjoy.

4. The series of enacted objectives are finally strung together in the actor's *through line of action*, or *through action*, which retains the sincerity of his emotional state while simultaneously exercising the detached control necessary to achieve the teamwork and unity of a play's performance. Olga Knipper as Masha in *Three Sisters* could say a dry eyed 'Goodbye' to her lover, but the impact of her total performance would bring tears to the eyes of those who watched her.

This kind of preparation for acting is hard and slow work, as patient and disciplined a way of life as that required of a musician, a singer or a dancer. There are those who believe uncritically that Stanislavsky's teaching has a universal validity, off the stage as well as on, and it is no doubt true that genuine emotions in the actor will result from the quality of his effort of understanding or feeling. However, Elizabeth Hapgood has reminded us in *Stanislavsky's*

Legacy that the master suggested the actor ask himself only '*If* I were Hamlet, or a tree, or a grand piano, how would I react?', and never to believe 'I *am*' Hamlet, or a tree, or a grand piano, unless he wished disaster upon himself.

11 *Chekhov's contribution to realism*

Uncle Vanya (1899), *Three Sisters* (1901),
The Cherry Orchard (1904)

The Moscow Art Theatre went on to produce the last plays of Anton Chekhov (1860–1904), each with a structure more fragile than that of *The Seagull* with its comparatively conventional plotting. These were Chekhov's masterpieces, *Uncle Vanya* (1899), *Three Sisters* (1901) and *The Cherry Orchard* (1904). Whereas Stanislavsky largely developed his thinking about the art of the theatre after Chekhov's death, it was during the production of these plays that Chekhov increased his understanding of stage realism. He learned by experience and largely taught himself.

Three Sisters was the first play he wrote knowing who might play the parts. This factor might be thought to make it easier to write 'to the life', but in practice the availability of a company who could be counted on to indulge his experiments presented him with the greater challenge. After seeing this play in rehearsal and performance, he continued to worry at its text to get it right. *The Cherry Orchard* gave him even more trouble. He cast and recast the parts in his mind, and the play was three years in the writing. However, he was a dying man by the time it was produced, and he was spared the work of rewriting it. As a result of his agonizing, his achievement was of such a stature as called for a redefinition of naturalism, and made Ibsen's look old-fashioned. Stark Young spoke for the post-Ibsen generation when he found that only Chekhov's plays as performed by the MAT gave him 'the thrill that comes from a sense of truth', for only they carried realism 'to an honest and spiritual depth and candour'.

Chekhov's comment on the actors of the St Petersburg *Seagull* had been, 'They act too much', for, like his contemporaries in the west, he was in full revolt against the popular drama and its style of acting. He was particularly incensed at the derivative nature of the traditional fare on the Russian stage: a French or German piece would be merely translated into Russian and have its characters' names changed accordingly. He also deplored the kind of false, external acting which went with this kind of shallow dramatic enterprise: after Bernhardt's visit to Moscow in 1881, he took even the divine Sarah to task, saying, 'Every sigh of Sarah Bernhardt —her tears, her death agonies, all her acting — is only a cleverly learned lesson. . . There's not a glimmer of talent in her acting, only a lot of hard work.'

At this time, the physical conditions of performance prevented any fundamental improvement. In a letter to his brother Alexandre of 20 November 1887, Chekhov described the opening night of an earlier play, *Ivanov*, in Moscow:

> Curtain rises. Enter the person for whom the benefit is
> being given. Diffidence, ignorance of the parts, presentation
> of the bouquet, combine to make me unable, from the first
> phrase, to recognize my play. Kiselevsky, on whom I placed
> great hopes, did not pronounce a single phrase correctly.
> Literally: *not one*. In spite of this, and the prompter's mis-
> takes, act ı was a great success. Many curtain cells. (Trans-
> lated Avialuu Tamollusky.)

There was little hope of an actor's catching the subtleties of the new dialogue when he expected to take a bow upon entrance before stepping into the action, and even then to stop to receive applause for his points throughout the scene. Nor was there much chance of conveying an ensemble quality in the portrayal of family life when each speaker drifted downstage centre to hear the voice of the prompter. Chekhov and his drama badly needed the reformed stage of the MAT.

In his last years Chekhov knew a little of Ibsen from Moscow productions, but he made it clear that he did not approve of Ibsen's kind of realism. Doubtless Chekhov recognized the forms and trappings of the well-made play still presented in the Norwegian: the big conflicts, the *scènes à faire* and the preconceived roles and attitudes, all lacking the quiet irony with which Chekhov himself saw human behaviour. He saw *Hedda Gabler* in 1900 and thought Hedda's suicide too sensational — 'Look here', he said to Stanislavsky, 'Ibsen is not really a dramatist.' At that time, Chekhov had already learned to write an objective, underplayed curtain scene. Even the most Chekhovian of Ibsen's plays, *The Wild Duck*, which Chekhov saw in 1901, he found 'uninteresting'. He saw *Ghosts* just before his death in 1904, and again the curt verdict : 'A rotten play'. It was Ibsen's lack of humour and his posture as a moralist whiich disturbed the Russian, whose aim was to keep his characters flexible and his mind open.

Chekhov himself pursued a unique objectivity in his naturalism. 'Freedom from force and falsehood, no matter how they manifest themselves', he wrote to his editor Pleshcheyev on 4 October 1888. He refused to moralize, and part of the discomfort of watching Chekhov on the stage comes of having no moral position to espouse. 'I have not introduced a single villain nor an angel, although I could not refuse myself buffoons; I accused nobody, justified nobody' (this in a letter of 24 October 1887). So it is that we can be angry with Mme Ranevsky for letting the orchard slip through her fingers, like the money we twice see her give away so recklessly, but we can also understand her inability to manage a situation wholly foreign to her nature and upbringing. The well-known assertion by Chekhov that 'a writer should be as objective as a chemist' (14 January 1887) could sum up the reasons why he goes beyond Ibsen and Strindberg in his realism. Chekhov had been trained as a physician, but his pursuit of a scientific ideal of truth, one in which the writer was required to be as impersonal as a doctor examining a patient, really came of his extraordinarily sharp eye for spotting incongruity in human behaviour. This kind of objectivity forced upon the audience a role equivalent to that of a jury presented with a mass of circumstantial and contradictory evidence — it must stand back and coolly sort it out.

By the time Chekhov wrote *The Cherry Orchard*, the last vestiges of romantic sensationalism had disappeared from his playwriting. There is no shot fired on or off the stage, no death of one of the characters to upset the balance of interest. Epihodov's pistol is all for laughter, and Charlotta's hunting gun amusingly illuminates her character. Every love scene in the play, Anya with Trofimov, Yasha with Dunyasha, Varya with Lopakhin, is designed for an incisive moment of comic irony. The triumph of Lopakhin, who becomes the new owner of the very estate where his family had formerly worked as serfs, is undercut by his drunken good humour, and any grand and knowing statement in his public announcement of the purchase in act III is not to be found. There is no villain, no hero, no moral, just a calm and amused treatment of a potentially enormous and explosive situation, that of the breaking up of the old order and the disintegration of a whole class of society. In form and style, *The Cherry Orchard* was a final rejection of the ways of the nineteenth-century stage and drama.

Chekhov had unwittingly prepared himself to become Russia's greatest playwright by writing hundreds of short stories to order: it was the kind of particularity and economy that could serve the stage well. The stringent requirement of no more than 1,000 words for each of his early stories taught him to work by a highly selective and impressionistic method, pruning ruthlessly at every opportunity. 'Brevity is the sister of talent', he wrote in a letter of 11 April 1889, and his stories are little jewels of compressed character and suggested situation. His regular advice to the new authors who regularly flooded him with their manuscripts was to avoid generalizations, acquire a glancing style of writing, and deal in fine details: observation and the study of actual life, he reiterated, were the essential pre-requisites of a good writer. So in *The Cherry Orchard* Chekhov discovered that a caramel popped into Gaev's mouth could illuminate the man's character in a flash, as well as neatly undermine what he had just said; or the brash handling of a Parisian cigar could indicate vividly that Yasha had ideas above his station, but knew how to flatter the servant girl sitting beside him even by puffing smoke into her face.

A richer, submerged life in the text is characteristic of a more profound drama of realism, one which depends less on the externals of presentation. In Chekhov's last two plays, the hints and suggestions are more minute and prolific, so that the spectator's attention to the surface clues becomes more intense: 'It is necessary that on the stage everything should be as complex and as simple as in life. People are having dinner, and while they're having it, their future happiness may be decided or their lives may be about to be shattered.' By applying this formula to *Three Sisters*, for example, we recognize the reason for Olga's horror at Natasha's ill-treatment of the old servant Anfisa from our sense of Olga's background; or we reach our own sceptical conclusions, from the youthful enthusiasms she displayed before, about Irina's ardent intention to earn an honest living; or we understand Masha's reluctance to pick up life again with her husband Kuligin from the abject pride he takes in his school and his headmaster.

Chekhov went much farther than Ibsen in providing suggestive settings for his plays, but without having any symbolic image intrude upon the realistic content. The progression of the scenes in *Uncle Vanya* takes us from outside the house deeper and deeper into the heart of the household, and finally into Vanya's own room — by which time his soul is bared. The sets in *Three Sisters* trace the dispossession of the family from the comfort of their drawing room to the confined action of act III in a bedroom, and finally in act IV to the garden outside the house, which is now occupied by the disposses-

13. Chekhov, *The Cherry Orchard*, Moscow Art Theatre, 1904. Production by Stanislavsky. Act IV, set by V.A. Simov.

sors Natasha and her lover Protopopov. In *The Cherry Orchard* we pass from the nursery, the one growing point for the life of the whole family, out to the orchard and a little beyond, almost to the fringes of a new industrial town, and then back again, as if to depict in the stage settings the cycle of the characters' existence, and perhaps the cycle of nature itself.

So, too, the weather and the seasons change significantly from scene to scene. The heat of a hot, humid summer afternoon in act I of *Uncle Vanya* reinforces the soul-destroying routine of life on the estate, until the storm breaks by act III and feelings spill out. In *The Cherry Orchard*, the chill of spring gives way to the warmth of summer, and then to the returning chill of incipient winter, suggesting a steady passage of time to match the cycle of the cherry trees from their blossoming to their destruction, as well as the change from hope to despair in the family. Meyerhold recognized afterwards that Chekhov's strength did not lie in such surface effects as the chirping of crickets and the barking of dogs; rather, the unique rhythms of his drama created a 'mystic lyricism' designed to feed the imagination of his audience.

Yet 'lyricism' is inadequate as a word with which to identify the Chekhovian drama. Just as the direction of Chekhov's art as a writer of stories was towards creative reporting, so his craft as a playwright was towards 'documentary'. His naturalistic ideal was to let actuality speak for itself without apparent manipulation or distortion for didactic purposes. In giving *Uncle Vanya*, the first of his wholly naturalistic plays, the subtitle *Scenes from Country Life*, he seemed to be declaring his new role as a descriptive recorder. This play like the one that follows it, essentially lacks a central figure, and by the dry and untheatrical way it opens and then has the title character slump on a seat dishevelled and yawning as if he had just rolled out of bed, Chekhov was challenging, if not insulting, the Moscow audience and its expectations. Judged at a superficial level, the play seems to take for a theme the problem of absentee landlordism, the poverty of rural Russia, and the indifference of the Russian intellectual, so that its author could be a kind of social historian. At quite another level, he tries to probe the nature of day-to-day living in all its triviality and futility.

Chekhov brought the same objective approach to the petty life of provincial Russia in *Three Sisters*, and to the world of *The Cherry Orchard* a sense of the pressure of social change. In a hundred tangential details Chekhov is the sly social critic gently pricking the conscience of his audience. There is no better example of this facility than when he obliquely touches the Jewish question in *The Cherry Orchard*. We hear the pathetic Jewish orchestra scraping together a living on two occasions in the play: once in the distance across the fields, and once after Mme Ranevsky has hired them to play at her unfortunate party. She betrays her feelings of guilt towards the Jews in so doing, and even though she cannot pay them ('Offer the musicians some tea', she says in a sorry voice) and we do not see them, the incident is a reminder of the persecution of the Jews under the Tsars.

In rejecting the traditional structure of interest and excitement in his plays Chekhov took an extraordinary risk. He set himself the task of presenting mediocrity, futility and boredom to his audience without boring it, and of making a broad, general statement without losing the particularity needed to make a sharp and realistic impact. Chekhov's documentary method supplied a strong compensatory element, however, by showing him a technique of full and engrossing character-drawing. He created memorable characters, not by working on some sensational, larger-than-life eccentricity, but by his unusual gift for observing people. His aim was to bring about an audience's understanding and conviction. In lieu of a strong plot and striking events, Chekhov placed weight on a character's motives: from the start, the sisters' dream of Moscow is as hopeless as the redemption of the cherry orchard, and so the audience is persuaded to examine the behaviour of these people under commonplace and recognizable stresses.

Audiences accustomed to the traditional control of an unfolding narrative and provocative action on the stage — the imperatives of 'What will happen next?' — were naturally troubled. Without a central character upon whom to focus attention and whose moral guidance to follow, they had little to hold on to. One sister would have been a convenience, but three were a distraction. These qualities, together with Chekhov's oblique way of presenting the human comedy without explicit social commentary, were unprecedented in modern drama. Even Tolstoy was deceived into thinking that

Chekhov lacked a governing theme or idea. For some playgoers, therefore, Chekhovian comedy has been relegated to the category of an acquired taste, for which an audience has to make a special effort of perception.

As for the actor, he is delighted to learn quickly that in the mature Chekhov play, every character has a complete life story embedded in his lines. Chekhov creates a rich and rounded character by supplying a hundred fragmentary impressions. And just as an audience has to decipher the code in the lines if it is to disclose the feelings and memories latent in them, so had the actor to decipher Stanislavsky's 'subtext'. The Chekhovian way with character was especially rewarding for actors who had acquired the skills of the Stanislavsky System: Chekhov never lets an actor down, and, like Shakespeare's characters, the larger parts are inexhaustible in their spectrum of possibilities. Even lesser semi-choric or background parts like Telegin, the guitar-playing parasite in *Uncle Vanya*, or the old nurse Anfisa in *Three Sisters*, invite the actor to contribute something of himself. No actor need feel like a supernumerary in a Chekhov play.

A singular problem for an audience watching a play by Chekhov, however, is to take in so large a group of highly individualized characters, for Chekhov habitually deals in whole families. Watching a play of his becomes an exercise in observing interactions and speculating upon interrelationships, constantly having to explain from the context of character and situation why something is said and done. In *Three Sisters*, Masha suddenly takes off her hat, silently indicating that she has decided not to leave; so we are compelled to seek the reason why she has changed her mind in what Vershinin has said or done. In *The Cherry Orchard*, Varya unexpectedly throws a pair of goloshes at Trofimov and, while it is true he is looking for them, she has no real reason to be so angry with him: we find the answer in her apparently unrelated disappointment in a character who is not even on the stage — Lopakhin, who has let her down again by failing to propose marriage to her.

The lack of focus on a single character after *The Seagull* is also compensated for by the proliferating patterns into which Chekhov contrived to have his characters fall. If his three sisters are each carefully contrasted in age and position, their attitudes nevertheless intersect at the mention of their old home, and they share a common nostalgia for Moscow. In *Uncle Vanya*, the characters fall easily into opposing parties of tormentors and victims, masters and slaves, and were it not for the ironic chorus of the Nurse, the old mother and Telegin, the melodramatic conflict of opposites would have been less muffled. By the time of writing *The Cherry Orchard*, Chekhov has subtly made each character at war with itself, so that a small cast represents a large variety of other discords — of youth and age, of financial solvency and insolvency, of contrasting social classes, of complacency and ambition, of marital needs. A few people become a microcosm of society, and introduce an unending complexity of interwoven thematic threads into the play. The patterns of accord and contradiction into which Chekhov's creatures fall increasingly affect the structure of rhythm and mood on his stage from moment to moment, and produce a new kind of 'poetic' drama.

Because of Chekhov's submerged character relationships, few other dramatists have demanded ensemble playing of such a high order. Epithets like 'orchestrated' and 'symphonic' began to creep into Stanislavsky's critical vocabulary, while discussion and rehearsal prior to a production took longer and longer. Today only a truly repertory company can blend the ingredients needed for a successful Chekhov production, for it takes time, not only to individualize character, but also to relate two or more such individuals : group acting can be convincing only if every character has drawn completely upon his history, and has developed an affective relationship with every other. And only if the group forms a unified whole can an audience assimilate the human values in the play feelingly. The implications of the Professor's announcement that he is going to sell the estate in *Uncle Vanya* touches every person in the family differently, and only the audience, perceiving the whole, can see how the proposal joins and divides each one, and how they support and fail each other in their moment of need.

Chekhov's method of juxtaposing individual attitudes in order to reveal an incongruous situation in its entirety is also one reason for his keen impact as a comic artist. Only by writing comedy did he maintain his objectivity in the face of the great social changes of his age, but his idea of the comedy suitable for a realistic play was by no means based upon the traditional exaggeration of character and the incongruity of situation. Chekhov's characteristic way of securing a balanced view was not to exaggerate but to undercut. *The Seagull* achieved this balance less well because it was constrained by the powerful ingredients of an earlier melodramatic form – in a realistic context, seduction and suicide are impossible to undercut. The relationships in the play are emotionally too intense, especially coupled as they are with the distracting suggestion of a conflict of innocence and evil among the principals. When Chekhov came to write *Uncle Vanya*, the feelings of Vanya, a man who has given twenty-five years of his life to a false idol, Professor Serebriakov, are certainly as intense as those of Konstantin Treplev, but the detachment of the audience is wonderfully secured when Vanya fires at the Professor and misses: the anticlimax of this incident in the third act, with the great man cowering in fear and the middle-aged rebel throwing a tantrum and casting aside his weapon in disgust, is irreducible by any comic evaluation.

Chekhov wrote comedy, yet comedy with a bitter aftertaste, again typical of his method. For we also *like* Vanya, and his cause is worthy. In a world where justice triumphs some of the time, Vanya

14. Chekhov, *Uncle Vanya*, Moscow Art Theatre, 1899. Production by Stanislavsky. Act III.

should have shot the Professor. The juxtaposing of pathetic and ridiculous incidents, the thrusting of farcical elements into a tense emotional situation, suppress any moralizing tendency and repeatedly induce the ironic detachment of the audience. It is this effect of distancing, together with the troubling relevance of his human and social themes and the elusive lyricism of his stage, which has made Chekhov an immeasurably pervasive influence on the form and syle of realistic drama in the twentieth century.

This is not to say that many modern plays or productions have been able to keep the infinitely delicate balance without which Chekhov's kind of realism amounts to very little as good theatre. The bulk of twentieth-century realistic comedy swings crazily between the grim and the giddy.

12 *Conflicts in Dublin: the Irish Dramatic Movement*

The Playboy of the Western World (1907),
The Plough and the Stars (1926)

Irish literary nationalism at the turn of the century was divided from the start. On the one hand was the loving desire to revive the heroic legends of Ireland's unhappy past, and on the other the need to represent the passionate purposes of the home-rule movement. The Dublin theatre became the centre of the literary awakening, a place where patriots could meet, and where the art of the drama could deal in folk-tales or politics, memories or prophecies. There the Gaelic League of Douglas Hyde, bent on reviving the Irish language and its culture, could quicken the imagination, and the nationalism of the Irish Literary Society could find a platform.

Irish dramatists writing for the London theatre have been the mainstay of English comedy since the seventeenth century: the distinguished company includes Congreve, Farquhar, Steele, Goldsmith, Sheridan, Boucicault, Wilde and Shaw. Their satirical wit, however, had done little or nothing for Irish drama itself. It fell to an Anglo-Irishman, William Butler Yeats (1865–1939), already an established poet, to promote a national Irish drama, this with the initial help of the writers Edward Martyn and George Moore. Yeats decided that the drama was the most likely form for stimulating a literary revival of wide appeal, and he was personally drawn to the folk imagination of the past — a factor which would have strange consequences. His lyrical verse play, *The Land of Heart's Desire*, had already been produced in London in 1894, but it was unknown in Ireland. A production of this rather sentimental piece at the Avenue Theatre, Dublin, in the same year could be said to mark the modest beginning of the Irish Dramatic Movement.

The journal of the Irish Literary Society, *Beltaine* (later, *Samhain*), at first urged those interested in the new cause to join in the advances being made in Europe. But at this time continental theatre was revolving round Ibsen and Ibsenism, and since Yeats did not much like Ibsen, the Irish movement did not follow the path of the Independent Theatres. Yeats had seen some of Ibsen's plays done in London by the Independent Theatre Society, and at first thought he had found the model for a theatre in Dublin. He could say at first that Ibsen was 'the one great master the modern stage has produced' and believed that 'we Irish' had 'far greater need of the severe discipline of French and Scandinavian drama than of Shakespeare's luxuriance' (*Plays and Controversies*, p. 12). But he had seen only Ibsen's social plays, and found them insufficiently poetic for his idea of a national theatre.

After seeing *A Doll's House* in London, Yeats reported some years later on its first night:

> I was divided in mind, I hated the play... I resented being invited to admire dialogue so close to modern educated speech that music and style were impossible... As time passed Ibsen became in my eyes the chosen author of very clever young journalists ... and yet neither I nor my generation could escape him because, though we and he had not the same friends, we had the same enemies (*Autobiographies*, pp. 343–4).

Again on *A Doll's House*:

> Ibsen has sincerity and logic beyond any writer of our time, and we are all seeking to learn them at his hands; but is he not a good deal less than the greatest of all times, because he lacks beautiful and vivid language? (*Plays and Controversies*, p. 119).

And after seeing *Ghosts*:

> At the first performance of *Ghosts* I could not escape from an illusion unaccountable to me at the time. All the characters seemed to me to be less than life-size; the stage, though it was but the little Royalty stage, seemed larger than I had ever seen it. Little whimpering puppets moved here and there in the middle of that great abyss (*Plays and Controversies*, p. 122).

He recognized that *Rosmersholm* had touched symbolism, but complained of its 'stale odour of spilt poetry'. He also saw the danger in the second-rate problem plays that followed in Ibsen's wake, and was determined to avoid what he considered to be middle-class theatre: 'It is always Shakespeare or Sophocles, and not Ibsen, that makes us say, "How true, how often I have felt as that man feels".'

In his Preface to *The Playboy of the Western World* in 1907, Synge would echo Yeats in criticizing the drama of Ibsen and Zola as 'dealing with the reality of life in joyless and pallid words', and in his Preface to *The Tinker's Wedding* in the same year, he argued that the drama did not have to reproduce problems to be serious; it was enough that it gave 'the nourishment, not very easy to define, on which our imaginations live'. So it was that Europe's Ibsenite impulse was scarcely felt in Dublin. It was left to the Gate Theatre after 1928 to pursue continental experiments with expressionism and other modes neglected by the Irish National Theatre.

The Irish movement was exceptional in being run by writers and not by actors, which may account for the quarrels that followed, and, in Denis Johnston's view, for its remarkable survival. Yeats's dream was of a 'people's theatre', one in which artists could return to the 'sources of art', Ireland's primitive mythology and its native speech, in order to create on stage 'that life of poetry where every man can see his own image'. In his way, Yeats was for both the truth of reality and the ideal of the imagination at the same time. In the *Boston Evening Transcript*, he said he sought both to represent 'a real life where men talk picturesque and musical words', and to show that 'our theatre of folk art is . . . an expression of the Irish mind of today'.

The next step was to agree a policy. Yeats met the influential landowner Lady Augusta Gregory (1852–1932) at her home in Coole, Galway, in 1898, and it was there in another historic meeting that they together conceived the idea of an Irish Literary Theatre based in Dublin. They drafted this manifesto:

> We propose to have performed in Dublin, in the spring of every year, certain Celtic and Irish plays, which whatever be their degree of excellence will be written with a high ambition, and so to build up a Celtic and Irish school of dramatic literature. We hope to find in Ireland an uncorrupted and imaginative audience trained to listen by its passion for oratory, and believe that our desire to bring upon the stage the deeper thoughts and emotions of Ireland will ensure for us a tolerant welcome, and that freedom to experiment which is not found in theatres of England, and without which no new movement in art or literature can succeed. We will show that Ireland is not the home of buffoonery and of easy sentiment, as it has been represented, but the home of an ancient idealism. We are confident of the support of all Irish people, who are weary of misrepresentation, in carrying on a work that is outside all the political questions that divide us.

This document is reproduced in Lady Gregory's *Our Irish Theatre*.

The reference to buffoonery and easy sentiment is to that unreal image of the stage Irishman and his activities which plagued the drama of the nineteenth century in the need for quick laughter. Maurice Bourgeois has usefully described in Jonsonian terms this 'Pat' or 'Paddy' or 'Teague':

> He has an atrocious Irish brogue, makes perpetual jokes, blunders and bulls in speaking, and never fails to utter, by way of Hibernian seasoning, some wild screech or oath of

Gaelic origin at every third word; he has an unsurpassable
gift of 'blarney' and cadges for tips and free drinks. His
hair is of a fiery red; he is rosy-cheeked, massive and
whiskey-loving. His face is one of simian bestiality, with an
expression of diabolical archness written all over it. He
wears a tall felt hat . . . with a cutty clay pipe stuck in
front, an open shirt collar, a three-caped coat, knee-breeches,
worsted stockings and cockaded brogue-shoes. . . His main
characteristics . . . are his swagger, his boisterousness and
his pugnacity.

In some of this we may recognize Sheridan's prototype for Sir
Lucius O'Trigger of *The Rivals*, and may be sorry to lose him. But
Yeats was taking a fundamental step in asking for a new degree of
realism. It can be readily seen from the manifesto how different
from the naturalistic theatre of Europe was the intention of the Irish
movement, but it nevertheless aimed at comparable ideals of truth,
and, like its European counterpart, wanted the chance to break
new ground in opposition to the commercial theatre. In the event,
the Abbey was the first successful English-speaking repertory company, even if run by writers and not by actors.

Yet, being run by writers, the new theatre was set about by
rules. In its early years, Yeats prepared a further document entitled,
'Advice to Playwrights who are Sending Plays to the Abbey, Dublin'.
This extract summarizes well enough Yeats's early ideas:

The Abbey Theatre is a subsidized theatre with an educa-
tional object. It will, therefore, be useless as a rule to send
it plays intended as popular entertainments and that alone,
or originally written for performance by some popular actor
at the popular theatres. A play to be suitable for performance at the Abbey should contain some criticism of
life, founded on the experience or personal observation of
the writer, or some vision of life, of Irish life by preference,
important from its beauty or from some excellence of style;
and this intellectual quality is not more necessary to
tragedy than to the gayest comedy.

We do not desire propagandist plays, nor plays written mainly to serve some obvious moral purpose; for art

seldom concerns itself with those interests or opinions that
can be defended by argument, but with realities of emotion
and character that become self-evident when made vivid to
the imagination ... A work of art, though it must have the
effect of nature, is art because it is not nature, as Goethe
said: and it must possess a unity unlike the accidental
profusion of nature.

Here again, Yeats clearly indicated the Society's rejection of the
conventional fare of the popular theatre. Here, too, he sowed the
seeds of dissent from naturalism.

In the 1904 issue of *Samhain,* Yeats went further, and declared
his preference for tragedy over social drama:

The arts are at their greatest when they seek for a life
growing always more scornful of everything that is not
itself and passing into its own fullness, as it were, even
more completely as all that is created out of the passing
mode of society slips from it; and attaining that fullness,
perfectly it may be — and from this is tragic joy and the
perfectness of tragedy — when the world itself has slipped
away in death.

It is good that in principle the movement should be national without
being nationalistic, but eventually Yeats's idealism, his desire for
a drama composed without restrictions upon the imagination,
will also eliminate character itself, and with it the human and social
element that was the stock-in-trade of the realists.

The first productions of the Irish Literary Theatre were put on
in the Ancient Concert Rooms, Dublin, in 1899. Yeats's *The Countess
Cathleen,* written in the manner of a poetic fantasy by Maeterlinck,
and Martyn's *The Heather Field,* an Ibsenite tragedy that had been
refused in London, were chosen to launch the new movement. They
were two plays which drew upon the Irish past and on the beauty
of Irish speech, but which represented uncomfortably conflicting
styles. *The Countess Cathleen* told the legendary story of a saint who
sold her soul for Ireland, and it was quite unlike Martyn's play. *The
Heather Field* reflected Strindberg as much as Ibsen, being about a
poor wife who felt she had to commit her husband to an asylum, in
spite of her need to support her children and herself. Realism and

romance sat uneasily side by side, and Yeats heard the first murmur-
ings of distrust. Next year at the Gaiety Theatre the same contradiction was felt, with Martyn's dreamlike *Maeve* set against his comedy
of local politics, *The Bending of the Bough*. This precarious arrangement persisted, with Irish myth rubbing shoulders with plays of
social commitment, until Martyn and Moore broke away to found
the Irish Independent Theatre with the intention of producing
despised European plays along with the native product. However,
the Literary Theatre had at least begun to build itself an audience,
if on somewhat parochial foundations.

These first productions were received with enthusiasm, although only English actors were to be had. As time passed, the Irish
actors W. G. and Frank Fay greatly encouraged the submission of
native plays when they reorganized the Literary Theatre as the Irish
National Dramatic Company, employing only Irish actors. The
year 1902 seemed to bring victory for Yeats's romantic theories
when his own *Kathleen Ni Houlihan* and A. E.'s *Deirdre* appeared on

15. The Abbey Theatre, Dublin in 1951.

the same bill. With Maude Gonne, the Irish patriot and beauty, playing the part of the lovely Kathleen who symbolized the spirit of Ireland, the direction of the Irish movement seemed assured. Then in 1904, an unexpected subsidy came from an English benefactor, Miss A. E. F. Horniman, a rich spinster, heiress to the family tea business. Annie Horniman guaranteed the company its own playhouse, which quickly became known as the Abbey Theatre. The Abbey was a tiny theatre, with a capacity of only 562 and a proscenium opening of only 18 feet, but in many ways it was just the right size to handle the intimate detail of realism and to excite those mutually patriotic feelings the movement wished to foster.

Certain other developments also offset the strongly poetic repertoire. Between 1903 and 1912, Lady Gregory herself for her own amusement wrote numerous one-act village comedies, including one or two tragedies. These little plays came closer to a realistic representation of Irish peasant life and speech than anything that had been written before. The best of them are *Spreading the News*

16. The stage of the Abbey Theatre, Dublin.

(1904), *Hyacinth Halvey* (1906), *The Gaol Gate* (a patriotic tragedy, 1906), *The Rising of the Moon* (1907) and *The Workhouse Ward* (1908). She also translated several comedies of Molière and Goldoni, done into 'Kiltartan' Anglo-Irish. Lady Gregory said that she had never cared much for the theatre, but the delight with which, in her middle age, she discovered that she could write plays is to be felt in her book, *Our Irish Theatre*. She experimented eagerly with themes and techniques, happily working out her ideas in practice and not in theory. The limitations of the company and the small stage also compelled her to exercise extreme economy in her stage planning; for similar reasons the original first act of Synge's *Playboy*, depicting Christy and his father in the fields, was later jettisoned, to the immense advantage of the play as a whole. In her study *The Irish Dramatic Movement*, Una Ellis-Fermor considered the influence of the live theatre on the written drama to be 'astonishing', and described how *Spreading the News* was conceived as a tragedy, but was turned into a comedy simply because that was what the Abbey needed to balance Yeats's verse plays.

Of greater importance, the plays of John Millington Synge (1871–1909) were written for the Abbey in its early years, and directed the movement along paths that Yeats could not have anticipated. Synge's talent as a playwright overcame all theories and all arguments, and the new impulse he started was continued powerfully after the war by Sean O'Casey — to the point where Yeats and O'Casey came into direct conflict.

Like Yeats and Lady Gregory, Synge was an Anglo-Irish Protestant, and his writing on behalf of a largely Catholic audience was consequently suspect to begin with. Controversy over his plays began with his first one-act comedy of 1903, *The Shadow of the Glen*, and reached its peak in 1907 with the week of riots that accompanied *The Playboy of the Western World*. No doubt the Irish enjoy the fun of making a disturbance in the theatre, but in this case an incident became a cause. In the New York production of *The Playboy* in 1911, rioting broke out again, and in Philadelphia the following year the company was actually arrested and put in prison. In Dublin, night after night the actors struggled on through the noise of the crowd and the pelting of vegetables. But those who came to hiss and boo at least paid to go in, and the Abbey grew relatively prosperous. Moreover, Synge's fame spread abroad, and with it the reputation of the Irish drama.

As it happened, Synge was an apolitical man, and unconcerned with Irish nationalism, but the violent reaction to his drama was the immediate result of the overheated feelings which surround the birth of any patriotic revolution. He had his share of Irish mysticism and feeling for nature, but the important truth was that he was the first major realist of the Irish movement. He drew directly upon the peasant life he had observed among the Aran Islanders, and was Ireland's first playwright to insist upon a certain critical honesty. There is little in Synge's plays which resembles the work of Ibsen or Strindberg, but in spite of Yeats they had subtly encouraged the new Irish theatre away from its insularity, and Synge was seeing his countrymen with the frank eyes of a realist who stood, as it were, well apart from their heated interests. Of course, in its narrower concern for the honourable image of Ireland, its Church and its womanhood, the Dublin public at the time was unaware of the quality and stature of the drama it saw.

In 'The Cutting of an Agate', Yeats wrote that Synge seemed

17. Synge, *The Playboy of the Western World*, the Abbey Theatre, Dublin, 1907. Act I, with Maureen Delayney, Arthur Shields and Sara Allgood.

by nature unfitted to think a political thought: 'In Ireland he loved only what was wild in its people.' But by now every Abbey play was closely scrutinized by Arthur Griffith's *United Irishman* and subjected to its militant journalese. Synge's first play, *The Shadow of the Glen*, drew upon the ancient farce of the young wife and the old husband who pretends to die in order to test her and spy on her. Nora, the young wife, does indeed have a lover in the traditional way, and as a result Synge was considered to have 'attacked the sanctity of marriage'. When applied to farce, such a comment is totally irrelevant, but loveless marriages and faithless wives have no place in nationalist sentiment. Blinded by this slight against Irish women, few saw that the story of Nora was never intended as a social problem, but, if anything, as a spiritual one. Behind the high spirits of the play lay Nora's fear of loneliness, as well as her desire to be free – a light view of the *Doll's House* situation. In vain did Synge protest in his Preface to *The Tinker's Wedding* that 'the drama, like the symphony, does not teach or prove anything', but the student of the Irish Dramatic Movement needs to study the political and religious assumptions of the Abbey audience to assess the truth of that.

The Playboy of the Western World tells the deceptively simple tale of Christy Mahon, a young farm lad of the Atlantic west coast. Christy has run away from home after he thinks he has killed his father with a loy in their potato field. He arrives at a shebeen run by Pegeen Mike, and there everyone assumes that he is running from the police. He soon becomes the hero of the village girls, and is delighted with his new reputation: 'Wasn't I a foolish fellow not to kill my father in the years gone by?', he asks innocently. His story of the loy swells with his glory, until his father, very much alive, arrives with a bandaged head and a foul temper. Now Christy is no hero at all, just the callow youth he always was, and the villagers turn on him viciously – they burn his leg – and throw him out. Dublin took this fantasy literally. How could patricide be so approved? Worse, how could a bachelor sleep under the roof of an unmarried Irish girl? The play was a travesty of both Irish womanhood and Irish manhood, nothing short of blasphemy against holy Ireland herself.

Judgment on the play's 'bestial depravity' and its 'malignant travesty of Irish character and of all that is sacred in Catholic life', as delivered by the Irish in Dublin, Boston and New York, strangely echoed the reception of *Ghosts*. Yeats's comment on the riots was that they were an outcry against the play's unsentimental way of seeing, 'a kind of sarcasm', as he put it. Synge had discovered his own mode of acid comedy by cutting down Pegeen's simple dream of 'a fine fiery fellow with great rages when his temper's roused' to the size of a simple-minded Christy Mahon, and placing at the centre the obvious but outrageous irony that the reality is not so impressive as the report. In fact, the reasons usually offered for the violence of the protest against *The Playboy* are not enough in themselves. No Irish audience could truly have believed that the oaths uttered by the characters constituted blasphemy – they were heard everywhere in Dublin. Nor did the city audiences really believe that the west coast peasantry was so noble, or so simple, that it would not provide cover for a murderer. The Dubliner may be an idealist, but he is not a fool. Yet no doubt he did perceive that Synge's manipulation of his fantasies was something of an insult, and we turn to the structure of the play itself, the way it works in performance, for clues to the real source of Irish indignation.

At the outset, Christy is a poor sort of creature and his deed is reprehensible by any code; yet he progresses to become 'a proven hero in the end of all'. Within this ironic framework, irony is piled upon irony as the audience rejects Christy, and then lends him grudging admiration, rejects and then approves the attitudes of those in the Mayo shebeen. By his mere presence, the snivelling coward Shawn Keogh constitutes a sarcastic comment on the situation, since the Pegeen's life partner he is the only alternative to a parricide. The miserable Shawn with his false piety is also apparently the Church's only answer in lieu of the presence of Father Reilly and the saints of God, all kept well offstage. When Pegeen's father, Michael James, tries to prompt Shawn to claim Pegeen for himself, Shawn can only whine that he is 'afeard to be jealous of a man did slay his da'. Which, for the audience, is reasonable enough, but no less vexing all the same.

Old Mahon himself is a second ironic presence lurking throughout the play, constantly undercutting Christy's heroic image by obstinately refusing to be dead. The audience is ready enough to grant the playboy some of the stage glory he has acquired by winning races on the beach, flaunting his colourful jockey silks and attracting all the young women in their bright red dresses (as authentically worn by the Aran peasant girls). He even pleases us by threatening Shawn's skull with another loy. But in the latter part of the play Old Mahon's sly presence is planted like a warning, threatening to thwart our pleasures. Nevertheless, Michael James himself accepts the idea that 'a daring fellow is the jewel of the world', even though he did 'split his father's middle with a single clout', and presumably may well do it again to a father-in-law; and so it seems, by dint of Synge's ironic stagecraft, that Christy's heroic image is solid and complete. When, therefore, Christy is finally chased off, threatening to kill his father a second time if necessary, the audience, as much as Pegeen herself, feels the pain and annoyance of self-deception.

Synge showed those on and off the stage how hollow is the fantasy of heroism upon which people feed, and not everyone who saw the first production was insensitive to the play's finely tuned comment on the Irish community. P. D. Kenny wrote in the *Irish Times* on 30 January 1907,

> I cannot but admire the moral courage of the man who has shot his dreadful searchlight into the cherished accumulation of social skeletons. He has led our vision through the Abbey-street stage into the heart of Connacht, and revealed to us there truly terrible truths, of our own making, which we dare not face for the present. The merciless accuracy of his revelation is more than we can bear. Our eyes tremble at it. The words chosen are, like the things they express, direct and dreadful, by themselves intolerable to conventional taste, yet full of vital beauty in their truth to the conditions of life, to the character they depict, and to the sympathies they suggest. It is as if we looked into a mirror for the first time, and found ourselves hideous. We fear to face the thing. We shrink at the word for it. We scream.

In other accounts of the production, there is little evidence of its quality, and perhaps we should assume that any element of farce or fantasy in the play was overlaid by the intimate realism of the Abbey performances.

Riders to the Sea (1904), Synge's little tragic masterpiece of Irish life and character, had been a safer play, the only work of his that the movement had accepted without question. *The Well of the Saints* (1905) was denounced, and the more anticlerical and inflammatory comedy *The Tinker's Wedding* (1907) was prudently never produced at the Abbey. Man cannot stand very much reality, said T.S. Eliot, and even realism of Synge's ironic variety, with locations far away from cosmopolitan Dublin, must be adjusted to its audience. Compromise may have been the chief reason for the subsequent decline of the Irish National Theatre over several years, but it took on new life after the establishment of the Irish Free State. At that time the movement had thrown up the vital early plays of Sean O'Casey (1880–1964), in some eyes Ireland's greatest playwright.

O'Casey offered the Irish National Theatre and its audiences a new set of challenges in *The Shadow of a Gunman* (1923), *Juno and the Paycock* (1924) and *The Plough and the Stars* (1926). His next great play, *The Silver Tassie* (1928), was the cause of a divisive quarrel with Yeats over its use of expressionism, and we shall therefore take up O'Casey's story again later (see vol. 3); but his decision to go into exile in Devon was a double disaster for the Irish movement and for the playwright, who continued to write plays for the rest of his life without the use of a native theatre to test and nourish his art. It is easy to see why his work was in fundamental conflict with the original ideals of the movement. Born in an urban slum, O'Casey knew the life of the city poor as none of his predecessors had. Could Irish folk-tales also include such people? There is nothing mythical or heroic about the back streets of Dublin. Involved in the dock strike of 1913 and in the street fighting of the Easter Rebellion of 1916, O'Casey was a Communist and an anti-Catholic, a realist with a cause, a passionate Dubliner writing for real Dubliners. In his best work he achieved a Chekhovian objectivity, infusing a grim drama of real events with an irrepressible Irish humour, and mixing comic and tragic elements in new ways to catch the full flavour of Irish life as he knew it.

The Abbey lost its momentum after the war because the new generation of Irish playwrights, like T. C. Murray and Lennox Robinson, was writing a more sentimental realism in spite of Yeats's original precepts. And when O'Casey began to write plays, he knew almost nothing of the Abbey and its traditions, and was too poor to have seen anything of Synge's work there. If he found a model anywhere, it was in the popular drama of Dion Boucicault (1820–90), whose effectiveness in the theatre he has been witness to, and whose plays seemed to work well both in Dublin and London, and on either side of the Atlantic. O'Casey knew many of Boucicault's more than 150 plays, and was especially familiar with those with Irish subjects, like *The Colleen Bawn; or, The Brides of Garryowen* (1860), which opened in New York, *Arragh-na-Pogue; or, The Wicklow Wedding* (1864), which opened in Dublin, and *The Shaughraun* (1874), in New York again – plays which expertly mixed comedy and suspense, but which only marginally touched the real Ireland. Therefore, when O'Casey put on a naturalistic stage the Dublin working-class he knew so well, he too appeared to be slipping into sentimentality by borrowing too many of the conventions of domestic melodrama.

The Shadow of a Gunman was received indifferently, perhaps because the play whetted the appetite for melodrama without satisfying it. Seumas Shields and Donal Davoren are a pedlar and a poet who share a tenement room in a Dublin slum, harassed by the typical landlord of melodrama. The beautiful patriot Minnie is in love with Davoren, and is shot in error by British soldiers. There is no heroic sacrifice in this story, and O'Casey's touch is present in making the patriotism seem hollow. *Juno and the Paycock* also draws on the stock situations of melodrama, this time the 'temperance' drama; his drunkard, Captain Boyle, is possibly modelled on Boucicault's character Conn in *The Shaughraun*. Melodrama dogs the family when his pathetic son Johnny is wounded in the hip and has an arm blown off in the fighting. Daughter Mary is an Irish beauty who attracts a sinister English lawyer named Bentham. She should have known better than to consort with the enemy, for in the last act we learn that she is pregnant and that Bentham has deserted her. No matter, Mary's loyal Irish boyfriend Jerry declares that his love for her is 'greater and deeper than ever'. Meanwhile, a legacy the family thought it had received turns out to be a mistake, and Johnny is marched off to a deserter's death at the hands of his former comrades-in-arms.

With such a plot, it might seem that nothing could redeem this

play from a watery grave. Yet O'Casey perversely makes his drunkard a comedian and his heroine something of a shrew: Boyle and
his wife Juno remarkably reflect the tough realities of Dublin life.
Then, when Jerry discovers that Mary is pregnant, we discover that
his charity does not extend to fathering another man's child. And the
play ends in total irony as Boyle and his drinking partner Joxer turn
Ireland's misery to ridicule. O'Casey has used the resources of the
old melodrama to attract his audience, and then has the uncomfort-
able capacity for laughing at us before we can laugh at him. His
sense of humour is unpredictable: when Mrs Tancred, one of the
neighbours, is burying her son, others are throwing a party. This
kind of irreverence was such that in the *Dublin Magazine* for March
1925 Andrew E. Malone complained that Barry Fitzgerald as Boyle
and F. J. McCormick as Joxer had 'played for laughter' at the
expense of the noble Sara Allgood as Juno. This was the O'Casey
touch, a new, ironic kind of realism, and it worked. In fact, *Juno and
the Paycock* was the greatest success in the twenty-year history of
the Abbey Theatre; performances were extended for a second week
and people were still turned away. In *Ireland's Abbey Theatre*, Lennox
Robinson considered that the play had rescued the Irish National
Theatre from 'artistic as well as financial bankruptcy' (p. 121).

O'Casey's first plays drew upon recent events in Ireland: the
Easter uprising of 1916, the troubles brought about by the Sinn Fein
in 1920 and the Civil War of 1922. So he was deliberately treading
on thin ice to begin with. His comic irony appeared to go too far with
The Plough and the Stars, which caused riots of the kind remembered
from the great days of *The Playboy*. In his book on O'Casey, David
Krause suggests that the play exposed 'the futility of Irish taboos —
religion, sex and patriotism', and certainly feelings about the
sacrifices of Easter Week were too fresh. The play even dared to
defend the victims of the fighting before the heroes, and bring the
sacred flag of the Republic into a pub. Irish womanhood was again
offended at Jennie Gogan's protest that each of her children 'was
got between th' bordhers of th' Ten Commandments', and by the
sight of a prostitute on the stage: an Irish girl a whore? The actress
Ria Mooney, who played Rosie Redmond, was warned that her
career would be finished. And then to see the woman plying her
trade at the same time as the patriot Joseph Plunkett proclaimed

the Republic from the Post Office steps! The play shocked the would-be, sentimental patriots mercilessly, those, in Peter Kavanagh's view, 'who imagine Ireland to be as green and level as a lawn, where the girls go around with eyes cast down, green garlands in their hair, and Rosaries at their girdles, while the men, armed only with shillelaghs, beat heavily armed battalions of British soldiers (*The Story of the Abbey Theatre*, p. 13).

Vegetables, shoes and chairs were thrown and stink bombs exploded. Some of the audience climbed on to the stage and tried to set fire to the curtain; fights started with the actors. O'Casey collected the ladies who were flung off the stage and started a discussion group by the stage door. Heated speeches were delivered, and Yeats himself harangued the house with the immortal announcement, 'You have disgraced yourselves again!' And afterwards the *Catholic Bulletin* damned the play as 'sewage school' drama. According to his autobiography, it is from this time that O'Casey began to feel a certain revulsion for the Irish theatre; he wanted to avoid being suffocated in an atmosphere so nationalistic and narrow. 'Sean felt a surge of hatred for Kathleen ni Houlihan sweeping over him', he wrote in *Inishfallen Fare Thee Well*. 'He saw now that the one who had the walk of a queen could be a bitch at times' (p. 186). The £100 award of the Hawthornden Prize for *Juno* at this time may have consoled him a little.

Nevertheless, the good old days of a realistic Irish drama seemed to have returned, even if as usual the heat of the occasion blurred the quality of production. Willie Fay and Maire Nic-Shiubhlaigh (Mary Walker), the Abbey's first leading lady, were the first to wrestle with the rhythms of the pseudo-Gaelic dialect Synge had invented after his visit to the west coast and transcribed without phonetic spelling. The importance of real dialect had never before been emphasized in a play to this extent, and now O'Casey was demanding authentic speech and behaviour. It was appreciated that the better the actors were, the more O'Casey's comic irony would hit home, and a first-rate Irish company was built up over the years. The Fays (William and Frank), Maire O'Neill (Polly Allgood), Sara Allgood, Arthur Sinclair, Barry Fitzgerald and F. J. McCormick were equal to the tones of a light, colloquial dialect, and could also catch the more sonorous notes heard occasionally.

Even if isolation from the mainstream of European realistic experiment did not help to advance the Abbey's techniques, they had the virtue of simplicity, derived from the small size of the stage and Yeats's reaction against fussy business and the over-elaboration of realistic detail. Writing in *Samhain* in 1902 of the production of A. E.'s *Deirdre*, he offered this advice:

> The background should be as of little importance as the background of a portrait-group, and it should, when possible, be of one colour or of one tint, that the persons on the stage, wherever they stand, may harmonize with it or contrast with it and preoccupy our attention. Their outline should be clear and not broken up into the outline of windows and wainscotting, or lost into the edges of colours.

At that time Yeats was thinking of a poetic stage, and arguing for a drama in which poetic language should be pre-eminent; his experiments in a symbolic mode would follow.

O'Casey's city realism was a far cry from Yeats's verse drama, yet he too would in time become a severe critic of realism. For neither Yeats nor O'Casey were Ibsenites, nor strictly romantics, and Yeats's limitations as a playwright were not such that he did not hold the art of drama well above the narrowness to which nationalism can reduce it. In the *Boston Evening Transcript* in 1911, George Moore wrote that while Yeats had 'no knowledge of the technique of the stage and no aptitude for learning it', and although he 'seemed the last man in the world who would succeed in running a theatre', he 'knew how to stoop to conquer, and he conquered, because he was possessed of an idea, and an idea is always sufficient to secure success'.

13 *Realism in America: Belasco to 'The Method'*

Until the twentieth century, the theatre in America remained largely derivative from its European cultural sources, and in the Victorian period it was dominated by the skill and invention of the Irishman Dion Boucicault and the theatre manager Augustin Daly (1839–99). Both of them worked on both sides of the Atlantic, thereby ensuring that the subjects and techniques of the native theatre were regularly fed and nurtured by its older cousins.

At the turn of the century, New York theatre was particularly enhanced by the achievement of David Belasco (1859–1931), a friend and disciple of Boucicault and a director strongly in the Victorian realistic tradition. However, unlike the naturalistic directors who were so much in rebellion against the commercial theatre in Europe, Belasco began as a stage manager within New York's commercial theatre itself, and was responsible for its best offerings in décor and scenic and lighting effects. Divorced from any revolutionary impulse towards naturalism in playwriting, his brand of realism cleverly misled an enthusiastic public into believing it was witnessing the development of the art of drama without the slightest challenge to its moral presuppositions. Belasco's actors were drilled with precision, and his stage excelled in spectacular mechanical invention. Indeed, his productions were distinguished by a care for technical detail which has been a characteristic of American professional theatre ever since.

Belasco himself wrote or adapted, sometimes with the help of others, many scripts which he thought would make good use of lavish realistic effects. He aimed at photographic accuracy. He experimented for months with the staging of *The Girl of the Golden West* (1905), for which he managed to reproduce the soft changing colour of a perfect Californian sunset over the Sierra Nevadas. For *The Governor's Lady* (1912), he set the stage with an exact replica of

18. Belasco production of *The Rose of the Rancho*, 1906.

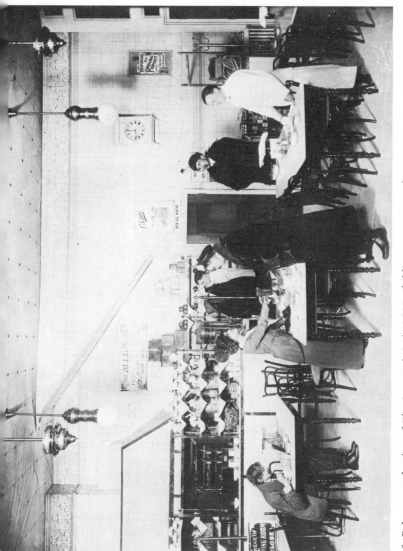

19. Belasco, production of *The Governor's Lady*, 1912. Child's restaurant on the stage.

Child's, a well-known Broadway restaurant. The scene of the ascent to heaven by Yo-San to meet her lover in *The Darling of the Gods* (1902) was achieved with breathtaking beauty by flooding a white set with celestial blue softened by gauze. For the noon heat of southern California in *The Rose of the Rancho* (1906), lights covered with yellow silk beat on a Spanish church, and the motionless scene, complete with a sleeping priest, a drowsy water-girl and two languid donkeys, held the audience spellbound for six minutes after the rise of the curtain.

If he brought unity and precision to the work of production, Belasco's appeal was first and last to the popular taste. At the time, a few believed him to be America's Antoine, but his autobiographical book *The Theatre through Its Stage Door* (1919) makes it quite clear that his vision did not go beyond a superficial idea of illusion. He claimed that the play is always the thing, and to this end he planned a scene, not by its author's stage directions, but to suit his own sense of its stage values. Those values were simple and spectacular: sunlight to suggest happiness, for example, moonlight for romance, gloom for tragedy, and so on. His constant object, he said, was to carry an audience 'back to its own experiences' and 'tug at the hearts'. His simple faith was that people went to the theatre 'to have their emotions stirred'. He worked from scenic models, lighting them meticulously for colour and atmosphere: 'Lights are to drama what music is to the lyrics of a song.' He had long since abandoned paint and flapping canvas; he believed in going to nature itself for a correct realism, and would send off an agent to France or Holland or Japan for authentic props. With all this, he was America's first autocratic director, dictating his conception of the play to his designer, his electrician and his actors.

The truth was, of course, that for all his brilliance Belasco perpetuated an out-dated realism, and one which would soon be excelled by Hollywood, and then replaced by the new stage arts we associate with Stanislavsky, Craig and Reinhardt. Meanwhile, a more urgent impulse towards realism was felt in the professional theatre. Having no independent theatre movement of its own, America was stunned by the sudden arrival of the naturalistic drama of Ibsen, Strindberg and Shaw. The less didactic Chekhov came later, and more indirectly, but finally more pervasively.

Ghosts had been presented in Norwegian as early as 1882 in Chicago, and in the same year *A Doll's House* was played in English in Milwaukee, mutilated under the title of *The Child Wife*. In 1887, *Ghosts*, encouragingly advertised as having been 'banned in Germany', toured the country as *Phantoms, or The Sins of His Father*, and in 1889, Beatrice Cameron played Nora in *A Doll's House* in Boston and New York. The London production of *A Doll's House* by Charles Charrington, with his wife Janet Achurch as Nora, visited New York in 1889. Then 1894 saw the American première of *Ghosts* in New York, with Ida Jeffreys as Mrs Alving. Thereafter New York was witness to a small procession of Noras: Minnie Maddern-Fiske (1894), Janet Achurch again (1895), the French Gabrielle Réjane (1895), the German Agnes Sorma (1897), Ethel Barrymore (1905) and the Russian Alla Nazimova (1908). Mary Shaw played Mrs Alving in *Ghosts* in 1899, and Nazimova in 1905. New York could not look the other way, and audiences were attentive, if uneasy.

In 1894 the first Shaw reached America; it was the deceptive *Arms and the Man*. In Arnold Daly (1875–1927), Shaw found an enthusiastic supporter, and Daly presented a series of Shaw's plays, including *Candida* and *Man and Superman*, before delighted audiences. All went well until 1905, when Daly dared to mount *Mrs Warren's Profession*, with the disastrous results that we saw (p. 60). It is not easy to explain why this play raised a riot in America as Ibsen had never done. It was at about this time that the critic George Jean Nathan (1882–1958) proved to be an important ally. A man of independent thought, Nathan made it his business to attack the sentimental theatre and pursue standards of taste and intelligence, which he believed he found in the new drama of ideas. He constantly brought the work of the leading European playwrights, Ibsen, Shaw, Hauptmann and Strindberg, to the attention of his countrymen, and in the avant-garde magazine *The Smart Set* saw into print the early work of America's first major dramatist, Eugene O'Neill.

The advent of Chekhov in America was much slower, but in the long run of greater importance; it is arguable that the characteristic realism in America is Chekhovian. Because of his close association with Stanislavsky and the Moscow Art Theatre, his impact on all aspects of the theatre in the United States was stronger than that of Ibsen, but his originality and obliquity as a realist took longer to appreciate, and certainly to imitate successfully. Chekhov's plays have the power of appealing to widely different talents, as is borne out by the use made of him in Britain by the two Irishmen Bernard Shaw and Sean O'Casey, even though their wit was of a different kind and their aesthetic founded on a different philosophy. Chekhov's influence in America, however, was more fundamental because it was felt through the practice of the theatre itself. This had not been the case in Britain, because the MAT's tour in 1922 had taken in Berlin and Paris, but not London. The turning point in America was the occasion of the MAT's visit to New York in 1923, where Stanislavsky's far-reaching autobiography *My Life in Art* was published in translation soon after in the same year.

News of Chekhov's success at the MAT, like his plays, was slow to reach America. When *The Nation* reviewed Julius West's early translations of a few of the plays on 13 April 1916, it found their theatrical value 'altogether inconsiderable':

> They are unfitted for general representation by their loose, haphazard construction, constant reiteration, excess of trivial talk and incident, manifest exaggeration, and mono- tonous drabness. The interest in them is almost exclusively literary and ethnical. . . Any attempt at a brief and intel- ligible synopsis of the rambling and invertebrate story [of *Three Sisters*] would be a mere waste of time and labor. The whole thing is suggestive of a collection of casual notes for an uncompleted novel of realistic impressionism. For the ordinary theatre it is utterly unfit.

Such views were not uncommon – even in Russia.

By the 1920s New York was becoming increasingly cosmo- politan, and foreign writers and artists were welcomed and ap- preciated. In October 1920, New York's avant-garde theatre magazine, *Theatre Arts*, edited at that time by Edith Isaacs, Stark Young and Kenneth Macgowan, devoted its entire issue to the organization, philosophy and methods of production of the MAT, which it declared to be 'the first theatre of the world'. In 1922, F. Ray Comstock and Morris Gest invited the MAT to New York, Chicago, Philadelphia and Boston for twelve weeks under Stanislavsky's leadership, since Danchenko had to remain in Moscow to work on opera with the MAT's musical studio. The Russians would be in New York in January and February 1923. In spite of the political mistrust between the USA and the USSR, articles everywhere began to appear in praise of the MAT and the quarter-century tenancy of its home stage.

The *New York Times* of 31 December 1922 invited the public to see the 'true picture of old Russia' and 'the finest dramatic art in the entire world'. Oliver M. Sayler wrote with wonder in the *New York Times Book Review* of 17 September 1922 of the lengthy rehearsals accorded each production, and of the training of new actors in the studio theatres. This at a time when standards on the Broadway stage were determined solely by commercial interests. He singled out the 'inner psychological and spiritual realities' achieved by Stanislavsky and Danchenko using these methods. Sayler also wrote the text for a lavish pamphlet in colour which was prepared for the visit, and in this he emphasized the pioneer nature of the MAT's achievement, noting that never before had America 'imported intact an entire dramatic institution of the prestige of the MAT'. Kenneth Macgowan had long been an advocate of the Russian methods, and in 1922 he published the influential book *Continental Stagecraft* in collaboration with the designer Robert Edmond Jones. In the editorial pages of *Theatre Arts* for April 1923, Macgowan drew attention once more to the virtues of the MAT's repertory system. In the United States, he believed, actors were cast 'piecemeal' according to their physical resemblance to the characters; but 'the heart of the MAT is the actor', who could play five or fifteen parts in a season to the great advantage of his art. He expressed the general amazement of the profession in America that it was the Russian custom to call for the opening night of a play, not on a predetermined date, but 'when ready'.

It was through this new interest in the Russian theatre that Chekhov received his major introduction to the American public. Under the headline 'The Russian Invasion' in *The Drama* for January 1923, Gregory Zilboorg declared that 'Tchekhov's drama is but another name for the Moscow Art Theatre.' The plays presented in New York in Russian were the MAT's crowning achievement: Alexei Tolstoy's *Tsar Fyodor*, Gorky's *The Lower Depths* and Chekhov's *Three Sisters* and *The Cherry Orchard*. The vitality of the productions prevailed over the audience's general ignorance of the language. Macgowan in *Theatre Arts* considered that the MAT demonstrated 'the perfection of an acting machine', by which the impersonations created were 'brilliantly exact and meaningful' and the plays presented were performed with 'almost infinite detail'. Stark Young, drama critic for *The New Republic* from 1921 to 1947 and probably the best of his generation, was less impressed by *Tsar Fyodor*, which he considered merely a showpiece of historical realism, but he found the Chekhov 'that rarest of events', a perfect combination of acting, production and playwriting. He invoked the phrase 'spiritual realism', which for him implied 'a selection among realistic details that can bring out the inmost spirit of the actual matter'. 'I saw Chekhov's art come true', he claimed, and said he experienced 'the thrill that comes from a sense of truth'. Stark Young continued to extol Chekhov for the rest of his life, and although Stanislavsky's Chekhov was the Chekhov of melancholy and disillusion and not the Chekhov of comedy and compassion, Young's advocacy must be accounted a factor in the Russian's continuing appeal in America. For the present, the tour in America was so great a success that the company was invited to return in 1924, and in the two years gave a total of 380 performances of thirteen plays in twelve major cities.

The flow of influential Chekhov productions in English began in 1926, when Eva La Gallienne's Civic Repertory Theatre on 14th Street played *Three Sisters*, with Miss La Gallienne herself as Masha. This fine actress deserves special mention, since she sacrificed a personal career on Broadway to form a repertory theatre for Ibsen, Chekhov and Shakespeare offered at popular prices. Broadway proper had to wait for its first Chekhov in English until 1928, when the pioneer English director J. B. Fagan presented *The Cherry Orchard* at the Bijou Theatre in George Calderon's translation. In his preface to the translation, Calderon had advanced a reason for the hesitation of British and American directors in tackling Chekhovian realism. He believed they were unfamiliar with his technique of 'centrifugal' action, in which the dialogue tended to fly away from the story line or central idea in order to illuminate the individual drama of minor characters. It was certainly different from the more narrative structure of the average realistic play in the Ibsen manner. Calderon argued in particular that English acting was ill-suited to a play in which the whole cast had constantly to remain 'alive' on stage, performing 'centripetally' in order to sustain the unity of the whole. In the 1920s, American acting was no doubt as inflexible as the British. At all events, the Fagan production compared badly with the MAT's of five years before: Brooks Atkinson, writing in the *New York Times* on 5 March 1925, found the audience 'drenched in boredom', with only gloom emanating from a 'cadaver' of a production.

Happily, the manner of realistic acting on the New York stage was shortly to undergo a sea change, brought about by a further influence from Moscow. The Polish-born Richard Boleslavsky (1889–1937) had been a member of the MAT from 1906, and he went to the United States in 1922. With Maria Ouspenskaya, another former MAT member, they founded the American Laboratory Theatre and began to teach the Stanislavsky System of acting. Among their students were Lee Strasberg, Harold Clurman and Stella Adler, who together were directly responsible for the radical change in the attitude and method of the professional actor in the United States. The Laboratory Theatre demanded new skills of concentration from its students, based upon Stanislavsky's method of developing an actor's 'affective memory', by which he could live an emotion over again.

The new realism also needed a supporting company and a home. The Provincetown Players had been started after 1915 by a group of New York artists who spent their summers at Provincetown on the tip of Cape Cod, where the first of O'Neill's plays were produced. Soon after, they opened the Provincetown Playhouse in Greenwich Village, New York, where they continued to present experimental theatre until they disbanded in 1929. These socially conscious years shortly before America's entry into the first World War also produced the Washington Square Players, another Greenwich Village enterprise, intent upon producing plays that were unacceptable to the commercial theatre. Forced to disband during the war, its members became the core of a more important organization in 1919, the Theatre Guild. For the first time the Guild operated on the subscription system, which ensured an audience for new and experimental plays, and in 1929 itself spawned the Group

Theatre, which for ten years determined the direction of the realistic movement in America. Much of the innovative theatre of the
1930s also derived from the economic depression which followed
the Wall street crash of 1929: the Federal Theatre Project and the
Theatre Union were especially devoted to a drama of social protest.
While these groups eclectically assimilated a wide range of new
styles, they particularly welcomed the new realism.

The Group Theatre achieved a notable consistency in realistic
production by training a permanent company in the Stanislavsky
System. In the Introduction to his *Collected Plays* of 1958, Arthur
Miller has testified to its quality: 'It was not only the brilliance of
ensemble acting, which in my opinion has never been equalled
since in America, but the air of union created between actors and
audience.' Some of the Group Theatre's directors, Cheryl Crawford,
Robert Lewis, Lee Strasberg and Elia Kazan, later worked with the
Actors' Studio with the explicit intention of giving the serious
actor intensive training in what became known as the American
'Method', a development from Stanislavsky's teaching. One of the
aims of the Group Theatre was to create a serious audience for a
serious creative endeavour, opposing the standards of Broadway,
and it is not unreasonable to say that this company has made the
greatest single contribution to realism in American theatre practice.

Harold Clurman (1901–   ) has told the full story of the
Group Theatre in his book *The Fervent Years* (1945). He was possibly
the most intellectual artist in the company, and he has been the most
articulate writer on the aims of a group trained in the realistic
method. He had seen the MAT in Paris in 1919, as well as in New
York in 1923, and he wanted in Italian the Russian professional
consistency in all departments of theatre, as well as in performance.
He also believed that the Group should express a clear purpose in
the choice of play to be produced, and that this purpose should then
be made visible in the way the script was interpreted. Clurman
gained a reputation as one of America's strongest directors in the
realistic manner.

Having also seen the MAT in New York, Lee Strasberg
(1901–   ) felt inspired to pursue his early interest in the theatre
more vigorously. Under the Russian influence he joined the Laboratory Theatre and helped to found the Group Theatre, staying with it

until 1937. With Cheryl Crawford, he directed the Group's first independent production at the Martin Beck Theatre in 1931. This was a play about decaying southern aristocracy reminiscent of *The Cherry Orchard*, Paul Green's *The House of Connelly*, with Franchot Tone and Morris Carnovsky. Although he tended to belittle as 'academic' the parallel with Chekhov, Clurman wrote enthusiastically of the production's 'acute awareness of human contradiction and suffering'. But Chekhov's influence was undoubtedly present.

More recent in this important line of realistic directors is Elia Kazan (1909–　). Kazan was a former member of the Group Theatre, and shared its interest in exploring social problems on the stage. He was also a member of the Actor's Studio, and shared its admiration of Chekhov. His directorial method therefore begins with Stanislavsky, and he injected into the realism of Method acting a quality of urgency and intensity of his own, alive with nervous energy. His work is today closely associated with the plays of Tennessee Williams and Arthur Miller, and Kazan was able to adapt his realistic techniques to support their impressionistic elements without difficulty.

The development of American realistic acting in the 1930s and 1940s was pronounced. The Actors' Studio was founded in New York in 1947, and Strasberg's name is particularly associated with

20. Paul Green, *The House of Connelly*, 1931. Directed by Lee Strasberg and Cheryl Crawford. The dinner scene, setting by Cleon Throckmorton, with Eunice Stoddard, Stella Adler, Morris Carnovsky, Mary Morris, Franchot Tone.

The Method he developed in his classes there. The actors who owe their individual style to him as a teacher make an impressive list: Julie Harris, Montgomery Clift, Marlon Brando, Eli Wallach, Paul Newman, Karl Malden, Kim Stanley, Geraldine Page, Ben Gazzara, Anne Bancroft and Shelley Winters are a few of them. It is interesting that these players are equally at home on stage or screen, where the intimacy of realistic performance is a special requirement. Strasberg's acting exercises were designed to bring out an actor's 'hidden personality', although there was some danger that an actor trained by The Method merely established his own personality at the expense of the character he was to portray. Nor could he so easily adapt his skills to any more 'presentational' style of acting appropriate to much pre- and post-realistic drama. In *The Paris Review* of summer 1966, even Arthur Miller spoke out against 'private acting', and was bold enough to say that Lee Strasberg was 'a force which is not for the good in the theatre', and Miller went on to say that 'He makes actors secret people and he makes acting secret, and it's the most communicative art known to man.' He was reminded, he said, of Walter Hampden's comment that some actors could, as it were, play a 'cello with perfect fingering, even when there were no strings on the instrument.

The British view of the American Method school of acting was fully expressed in a notable article by Tyrone Guthrie in 1957, 'Is There Madness in The Method?', which discussed its limitations. Guthrie faulted The Method on the grounds that it was 'in rebellion against conditions which have ceased to exist and, consequently, is out of date'. It also placed 'too much emphasis upon self-analysis and too little on technique. The work of the group, The Method, he argued, was an expression of American nationalism, a youthful revolt against a social situation, just as the MAT had rebelled against the theatrical *status quo* before it. Its plays needed to make heroes of taxi drivers and boxers, on the assumption that it was more 'real' to be rough than genteel. Coinciding with the popular impact of psychoanalysis, The Method believed that an actor could be better by Being Himself, which was a cliché 'inadequate to express any wide range either of character, environment or style'. Particularly if his voice remained his own, such a policy would be unlikely to 'take an actor far on the way to King Lear, Andromache or Faust'.

The sensible pursuit of craftsmanship was essential. The answer to Guthrie, of course, is that even the best craftsmanship may not be enough for Lear, Andromache or Faust, especially if the craft itself is cliché. Strasberg has made a valuable contribution, but the best way to become the complete actor is still an open question.

Strasberg directed a celebrated production of *Three Sisters* for the Studio in 1964, a real test of The Method in practice. However, Georgii Tovstonogov was not alone in finding it obsessed with detail, like a museum-piece. It was directed as if Chekhov were 'a mere annotator of manners', and Tovstonogov reported in *The Drama Review* for winter 1968,

> Lee Strasberg became, in my opinion, a victim of the tradi-
> tional idea of Chekhovian theatre. His *Three Sisters* was a
> collection of the most prevalent acting and directorial
> clichés. His stage was filled with everyday reality, done
> with photographic authenticity and combined with pro-
> tracted rhythms. There was no room for Chekhov's imagery.

The term now current to describe fussy realism is the uncomplimentary word 'literalism'. It is easy to understand how Chekhov's half-articulate characters lent themselves to the licence of The Method: the actor found himself working more with the subtext than with the text. In a lecture of 1957, 'America's New Culture Hero', reprinted in his collection *The Third Theatre*, Rubert Brustein laid down the warning that 'the subtext can be a stratagem by which the actor ignores the playwright's meaning, substituting the feeling he himself finds to be more compelling'.

Experiments with realistic performance styles meant that by the end of the 1920s the American theatre scene was set for uncommon advance in new, indigenous playwriting, in which the new realism would inevitably dominate much of the achievement. The actors were there, the skills were being learned, young directors were gaining experience. Above all, the time was ripe for a drama which declared a social consciousness and proposed a home-grown American theme. In reviewing a production of *The Seagull* for *The New Republic* on 9 October 1929, Stark Young made a remarkable prophecy:

> Of the important European dramatists, Chekhov is at

present the one who can be of most use to us. The technique of Ibsen is by now absorbed everywhere into modern playwriting, in so far as an insistent technical method, as divorced from the moral seriousness behind it, can be absorbed. At the other extreme, the poetic method seems far off from what is being thought for the stage. Chekhov's is of them all, the method most profoundly available to our uses. Without more management or stylization than we employ, without more removal or traditional manner than we practice, his realism has the same world as our realism, the only world our art knows for the present. What Chekhov can give us is plain. More delicacy of perception, more deeply interwoven themes, more subtlety of feeling, more poignancy, sincerity and truth of intention. For our American dramatists of today he affords the closest great influence to be had.

The influence was felt. Sometimes it is acknowledged, sometimes it can be inferred. Sometimes the links in the chain become too many to be more than tenuous. But, while other symbolist and expressionist dramatic experiments are tried, and vigorously, it remains true to say that every major playwright of the modern American theatre was touched at some time by Chekhov, Stanislavsky or The Method, and sometimes by all three.

14 Realism in America: early variations

Street Scene (1929), *Long Day's Journey into Night* (1956)

Elmer Rice (1892–1967) may be best remembered for his satirical and expressionistic drama, especially his parable of the machine age, *The Adding Machine* (1923), but in fifty years of playwriting he wrote over fifty plays in many different styles – even 'Living Newspaper' scripts at the time when he was involved with the Federal Theatre Project. If a streak of sentimentality vitiates his social and political drama, he created a rich variety of ethnic character studies, and had the ability to set these in a firm naturalistic frame. This he did particularly well in *Street Scene* (1929), one of the first American plays to experiment with the new realism.

Street Scene placed on the stage an actual environment, the façade of a city tenement building in New York, thus fixing the motif of the play as the life of the poor living in the city slums. It was a play, its first designer Jo Mielziner said, of 'almost journalistic realism'. As many as fifty characters of different national and racial origins – Irish, Jewish, Italian, German, Swedish and many more – inhabit the street and the building, and in numerous little 'sub-plots' they gossip, quarrel and joke with one another. It is an early summer New York heatwave, and all the windows are open and the people have spilled into the street. Noises of the city are punctuated by the screams of a woman in labour. A husband surprises his wife with her lover, and kills them both – a melodramatic incident which perhaps mars the play's sense of authenticity. Otherwise, *Street Scene* captures an image of life as it follows its dull and squalid day-to-day rhythms. The continuity of being alive is felt particularly strongly at the curtain, when a new couple enquires about the vacant rooms,

21. Elmer Rice, *Street Scene*, New York, 1929. Setting by Jo Mielziner.

the unchanging voices of children sing offstage 'The farmer in a dell', and a sailor crosses the stage with his arms round two girls.

Along with other managements, the Theatre Guild rejected this play as being undramatic and having no content. Rice finally produced it himself, and told the story of his difficulties in the chapter 'The Biography of a Play' in *The Living Theatre* (1959). Yet *Street Scene* ran for 601 performances in New York alone, and for six months in London; it was subsequently made into both a film and a musical. As drama, it had clearly touched a familiar nerve. The *New York Times* of 11 January 1929 was typical in finding the story of the play slight, but the whole production 'extraordinarily authentic'. It was impressed by the play's background of an 'average street' with people hanging out of windows on a hot night, and by the street life of policemen, postmen, babies, dogs being exercised, and 'the airing of night clothing in the faint sunlight of the listless city morning'. The business of 'merely living' was truly caught: 'the primitive facts of child-birth on the third story, the chicken for soup, the petting after dark, the common hatred of the intellectual Jew, race prejudices, class morality, jolly, broad humor, sympathies, jealousies'.

Elmer Rice knew his Chekhov intimately, and believed that the Russian did not depict reality, but rather 'the illusion of reality', in which 'the inspired use of a significant phrase may be more revealing than pages of transcribed stenographic notes', and 'the seemingly casual and rambling conversation' of Chekhov's characters had the cumulative effect of making us aware of 'their minds, hearts and souls'. Rice visited the USSR in 1932 and 1936, at a time when there was more Chekhov produced in New York than in Moscow, and reported that a Russian acquaintance lightly commented that Chekhov seemed to be the American national hero.

The depression years of the 1930s are associated with a drama of social protest, even of propaganda, and they also belonged to the realistic tradition. In 1934, the left-wing Theatre Union presented a militant play called *Stevedore* by George Sklar and Paul Peters, dramatizing an ugly encounter between black workers and the armed thugs of their employers, with the subsequent shift of sympathies by the whites in favour of the blacks. This sounds unrelievedly didactic, but the story was told with life and not a lesson in mind, so that particular scenes, like that of the black dockers laughing and quarrelling in the lazy noon sunshine among the bales of cotton, came across like the real thing. In the same year, the Theatre Guild presented John Wexley's angry play *They Shall Not Die*, a courtroom drama which re-staged the notorious Scottsboro trial of black youths as tried by southern whites. The play treated its subject with a deep conviction of truth.

Designers of such plays of social realism, like Mordecai Gorelik, would always research the actual locale of the play, whether it was a street or a dockyard, a farm or an iron foundry, and then attempt to create the idea as well as the atmosphere of the subject in the setting they designed. Gorelik eschewed abstract symbolism in his scenes, but spoke of creating the 'battleground' of the reality he sought, what he thought of as the play's 'dramatic metaphor'. But design conceptions were essentially realistic, and John Gassner has pointed out that the whole social-critical, semi-political movement in the American theatre was rooted in realism, even if it occasionally carried its audiences 'beyond realism' to more expressionistic realms.

In the 1930s the Group Theatre encouraged new American playwrights to work in the realistic vein, and of these Clifford Odets (1906–63) is one of the most interesting. His theatre career

22. Clifford Odets, *Waiting for Lefty*, Group Theatre, New York, 1935. Directed by Clifford Odets and Sanford Meisner.

began as a Group actor, and he developed his literary gifts with a strong sense of the social role of the theatre in the aftermath of the depression. The Group's notably youthful production of Odets's long one-act play *Waiting for Lefty* (1935), an 'agitprop' play of a superior kind, was basically expressionistic and episodic in structure, but the dramatic frame provided by the strike committee of militant taxi-drivers (New York had seen a taxi strike the year before) allowed for a series of five flashbacks done in the realistic manner. With a few simple props on a bare stage, each episode enacted an incident from the past experience of one of the strikers, creating a counterpoint of styles which was to become common in American avant-garde drama. However innovative, the concoction of *Waiting*

23. Clifford Odets, *Awake and Sing!*, Group Theatre, New York, 1935. Directed by Harold Clurman, setting by Boris Aronson.

for Lefty was extraordinarily effective: it is reported of the first performance that when the actors at the final curtain called out in unison, 'Strike!', the audience enthusiastically echoed them.

In the same year, Odets offered a play of almost total realism. This was *Awake and Sing!*, directed by Harold Clurman for the Group, and it clinched Odets's reputation as their most promising play-wright. In mixing tragedy and comedy, the play followed the techniques of Chekhov and O'Casey, although in construction the play is 'well-made' in the manner of Ibsen and the nineteenth century. It portrays a Jewish family living in the Bronx district of New York at the time of the depression, and the family's quarrels about money are noisy and human. Bessie Berger, the mother, is a

L to r: John Garfield, Morris Carnovsky, J. Edward Bromberg, Stella Adler, Luther Adler, Sanford Meisner, Art Smith.

domestic tyrant who at least ensures that the family survives and pays the rent. However, she at last resorts to marrying off her pregnant daughter to a wealthy man she leads to believe is responsible for the baby, and to keeping her son from marrying the girl he wants and leaving home. The crisis of the play arrives when Bessie's deceptions are recognized for what they are. In *Awake and Sing!*, the stage is alive with the turbulent life of the characters. Only its curtain speeches, which are tinged with propaganda, betray the objectivity of one of the best realistic plays of the period, and tempted the *New York Times* of 20 February 1935 to pronounce Clurman's direction 'overwrought and shrill'.

Odets's more tragic *Golden Boy* (1937), directed by Clurman at the Belasco Theatre, was its author's biggest financial success. Its central character is an Italian-American, Joe Bonaparte, and the action of the play develops as a psychological exploration of his mind and spirit. But the play is not merely a psychological study:

24. Clifford Odets, *Golden Boy*, Belasco Theatre, New York, 1937. Directed by Harold Clurman. L to r: Phoebe Brand, Lee J. Cobb, Will Lee, Frances Farmer.

it implies a powerful criticism of economic society. When Joe chooses the remunerative career of a boxer over that of a violinist, no doubt the unlikely symbolism of the choice hurts the realism of the character, but as Joe changes from a repressed youth to an arrogant prize-fighter who finally kills his opponent in the ring, the steady coarsening of the man we knew in the beginning makes for Odets's best study in human nature.

The Marxist impulse behind Clifford Odets's plays tended to make them thesis plays in the late Victorian manner, showing the poor and weak exploited by the rich and powerful. But if his flair for the New York idioms in speech and manner was sometimes self-conscious, it also made him the American playwright with the most unfulfilled promise of the decade. In *The Fervent Years*, Harold Clurman discounted Chekhov's influence on Odets, who, he said, knew little of Chekhov's work at this time. Nevertheless, in the year of *Awake and Sing!*, some members of the Group thought Odets 'the nearest thing' to Chekhov, and Odets himself wrote a publicity article, 'Some Problems of the Modern Dramatist' (later reprinted in the *New York Times* of 15 December 1935), in which he specifically rejected Ibsen as his mentor, and said he thought of himself as Chekhovian — a judgment which he later half-withdrew, perhaps to spare his own blushes. At all events, the question to be asked about *Awake and Sing!* is whether it could have been written had the Russian not existed. Odets perfected a dialogue of seemingly irrelevant and unrelated lines, which nevertheless showed how a family was bound together inseparably, and nothing quite like it had been written in English before.

In 1939, the Group Theatre adopted the exuberant San Francisco writer William Saroyan (1908—). Robert Lewis directed Saroyan's *My Heart's in the Highlands*, a rural fantasy which mixed its stylization with realism, and touched its vivid crowd scenes with good moments of realistic writing. In an article, 'Form in Production', Lewis described how he staged the moment when an old trumpet-player so enchants a group of Armenian-American villagers that they bring him food in their gratitude. The scene was based, Lewis said, upon the image of 'a plant flowering as it is watered', and he arranged the crowd below the old man and holding up their gifts to him 'as if they were growing

out of the branches of a large tree'. This is clearly a poetic treatment
of the scene even though Saroyan believed his play to be wholly realistic, and did not approve of his director's imaginative effects. Which
goes to show that one man's prose is often another man's poetry.

Saroyan followed this immediately by probably his best play,
The Time of Your Life (also 1939). Although initially rejected by the
Group as too formless and self-indulgent, this play was successfully
produced by the Theatre Guild. Its plotlessness was in fact intended
to suggest the life it aimed to represent. Brooks Atkinson found it
to be 'a reverie in a bar room, without much story and none of the
nervous excitement of the theatre'. Then he added, 'Nothing holds
this sprawling drama together except Mr Saroyan's affection for the
tatterdemalions who are in it. But his affection is no casual
sentiment. It has the force of a genuine conviction about people'
(the *New York Times*, 26 October 1939). This time Saroyan had
chosen an urban setting, where Nick's waterfront saloon in San
Francisco is peopled with types, 'a kindly saloon-keeper, a street-
walker with dreams, a colored musician, an aspiring tap-dancer, a
fabulous teller of tall tales, a worried cop, a boy in love, a crazy
Arab lounging in the corner'. Unfortunately, Saroyan's loose, warm-
hearted philosophy was ill-suited to the ominous year of 1939.

In this period, naturalistic novels comfortably assumed the
acceptable style of the new realism when they were adapted for the
stage. John Steinbeck (1902–68) successfully dramatized his novel
Of Mice and Men (which in any case had been first conceived as a
play) immediately upon publication in 1937, and caught the
socially-critical spirit of the decade without neglecting the virtues
of a particular story. A play about two itinerant farm workers in
southern California, it is a warm and sympathetic psychological
study of a simple-minded giant and his friend, who together dream
of the 'little place' they hope to own, until personal disaster over-
takes them. Their dream was echoed by audiences everywhere. In
1942, Steinbeck also dramatized his anti-Nazi novel *The Moon Is
Down.*

Possibly the most interesting adaptation was that of the novel
The Member of the Wedding, published in 1946 by the southern
writer Carson McCullers (1919–67). With the encouragement of
Tennessee Williams, who was also from the south and who had had

two recent successes on Broadway, McCullers's play was produced in 1950 by Harold Clurman. This play was a true challenge to Clurman's sensitivity as a director in the realistic manner. It tells the gentle story of an adolescent girl in Georgia, eager for her first glimpse into the adult world, and the play called for a Chekhovian technique in order to evoke the inner feelings of so delicate a subject. Julie Harris, a Method actress, played the motherless twelve-year-old tomboy Frankie, talking to strangers, or to the cat, suddenly 'flying' through the room as if round the world, trying a cigarette, treating familiar objects as if they were strange, twisting and turning as she begins to feel her sexuality, pathetically in love with the idea of her older brother's wedding about to take place in the house – to the point of her actually wanting to join the bride and groom and go away with them on their honeymoon. Clurman noted that when Frankie sobs aloud in the first act, the sound comes as the climax of all the many little symptoms of her loneliness.

In his production, Clurman created a human environment for Frankie by setting her among other people whose traits were equally individualized: the prosaic compassion of the cook Berenice Sadie Brown, as played by Ethel Waters, and the childlike indifference of the young boy John Henry, played by Brandon de Wilde, who runs busily in and out of the play. These three are confined in the kitchen of the house in which the big event of the wedding is to take place offstage. The reviewers agreed that *The Member of the Wedding* had scarcely any plot, or even character development, but that it had created an extraordinary mood – in the words of Richard Watts of the *New York Post*, 'a strange, haunting and delicate kind of rueful beauty' (6 January 1950).

Although unconnected with the Group Theatre, the earlier, socially-orientated plays of Lillian Hellman (1905–) contributed to the purposeful nature of the best American theatre of the 1930s. In 1934, she wrote the challenging lesbian play, *The Children's Hour*, in the Ibsen tradition of psychological realism. Her best-known play, *The Little Foxes* (1939), a study of greed in a southern family during the 'Reconstruction' after the American Civil War, was also in the 'well-made' tradition as a suspense melodrama. *Watch on the Rhine* (1941) was a realistic indictment of the Nazi régime. But she made an extensive tour of Europe and Soviet

Russia in 1936 and 1937, and the success of *The Little Foxes* and *Watch on the Rhine* in Moscow resulted in an invitation to her to visit Russia again late in 1944. The next major direction her playwriting took was Chekhovian.

Hellman's *The Autumn Garden* was directed by Harold Clurman in 1951, and both in its subject and the texture of its dialogue the play proved to be more like Chekhov than Ibsen. It was a subtly poignant picture of a group of decadent middle-aged people, all living with a sense of failure in a shabby southern boarding-house on the Gulf of Mexico. The play was witty and astringent, if lacking the characteristic Chekhovian warmth: Clurman has since called its comedy 'acrid', and its author 'hard-headed'. In their reviews, many critics remarked the presence of a 'Chekhovian mood', that is, finding it brooding and sombre. John McClain, writing in *The Journal American* for 8 March 1951, particularly perceived 'a distinct note of Chekhov sounding through the proceedings ... I would not have been surprised to hear those woodsmen hacking at the cherry trees as the final curtain fell.'

Hellman was a lifelong admirer of Chekhov, and she edited a popular selection of his letters in 1955. In her introduction to this book, she expressed anger at the presentation of Chekhov's plays that made him out to be a man who wept over the fate of 'sweet, soupy, frustrated people ... puff-ball people lying on a dusty table waiting for the wind to roll them off'. On the contrary, she believed Chekhov to be 'a tough, unsentimental man with a tough mind', an opinion which may account for the tough, unsentimental tone pervading *The Autumn Garden* and another play of decaying south-ern life, *Toys in the Attic* (1960). It is fair to say that good opinion of Hellman's work has steadily grown since the war, and the time may now have come for a reassessment of her place in the realistic movement as a whole.

Eugene O'Neill (1888–1953) was America's foremost dramatist during the first half of this century, a playwright ready to try any device, convention or style from the history of the theatre past past or present. After his early half-naturalistic, half-symbolic one-act plays about seafaring drifters in the play cycle *S. S. Glencairn* (1916–18), he was so influenced by the avant-garde critic Kenneth Macgowan and the designer Robert Edmond Jones in their endeavours at the Provincetown Playhouse that he did not consciously consider a less melodramatic style of realism until the end of his career. He was convinced that Strindberg was 'the precursor of all modernity in our theatre', not only for symbolism and expressionism, but also for a heightened naturalism designed to express 'inner spiritual forces'. Certainly O'Neill's pursuit of what he called the 'big feeling for life' suggests that Chekhovian realism is the wrong place to look for the origins of his realistic style, and for most of his career he deliberately turned instead to 'the opposite of the character play' — the expressionistic play, which will be discussed in volume 3. Yet in the *New York Herald Tribune* of 16 November 1924, O'Neill found Chekhov to be the writer of 'the most perfect plotless plays', and, fifteen years later, he finally abandoned his kaleidoscopic experiments with convention and in his last years wrote three major plays in a quasi-autobiographical and realistic vein that suggest that he had at last found his natural style. These great plays are *The Iceman Cometh* (written 1939, produced 1946), *Long Day's Journey into Night* (written 1939–41, produced 1956) and *A Moon for the Misbegotten* (written 1941–3, produced 1947).

With echoes of Gorky's *The Lower Depths* in its patterning, *The Iceman Cometh*, a play of nearly five hours' playing time, distributes about the stage nearly twenty characters, the derelicts and prostitutes who inhabit Harry Hope's waterfront saloon in 1912. The dialogue dips into pessimism as each character has his lifelong illusions smashed. Yet this grim play is less like Gorky and more like Chekhov in that its plot is negligible and inconclusive, with its characters tracing a theme only by their half-humorous interactions. Eddie Dowling directed the play at the Martin Beck Theatre, New York, with Dudley Digges as Hope and James Barton as the intruder Hickey, and those critics who found this production profound also found it long-winded. Directed by José Quintero ten years later at the Circle in the Square, New York, the play made the name of Jason Robards, Jr in the part of Hickey, and a better production forced a revaluation of its merits as a theatrical *tour de force* in sustained realistic atmosphere.

O'Neill had ceased to make concessions to his audience's span of attention, and the sharing of pain was also an unacknowledged, Strindbergian principle behind *Long Day's Journey into Night*, a play of greater stature. This was wholly autobiographical, and portrayed, as realistically as its author knew how, his own family remorselessly at war with itself. Like *The Iceman Cometh*, the play was also set in the year 1912. The pathologically parsimonious James Tyrone has driven his wife Mary to drugs, and his elder son Jamie to drink and dissoluteness; the younger son Edmund is suffering from tuberculosis. Family life is portrayed with complete conviction, but a greater 'reality' lies below the surface of the illusion: the four-act division of the play traces their life

25. Eugene O'Neill, *The Iceman Cometh*, Martin Beck Theatre, New York, 1946. Directed by Eddie Dowling, with James Barton as Hickey.

from morning to night, and this pattern outlines the shape of their anguish, with hope turning to anxiety, and night bringing despair — the pattern of tragic life itself. The play has been called a 'saga of the damned'. If its ending is melodramatic by modern standards, it is also powerfully moving, as the mother under the influence of morphine is suddenly heard playing the piano before she appears carrying her old wedding dress. Exhausted but sleepless, the men pour another drink while she recounts her memories as in a dream. The curtain falls on her lines, 'Then in the spring something happened to me. Yes, I remember. I fell in love with James Tyrone and was so happy for a time.'

O'Neill did not want so personal a play produced, but when it received a successful production in Stockholm in 1956, and when Quintero's *The Iceman Cometh* did so well on Broadway, O'Neill's widow permitted him to direct *Long Day's Journey* in the same year. While London was beset with 'angry young men' and *Look Back in Anger* in 1956, New York was rediscovering its greatest dramatist, an angry old man. The notable cast had Florence Eldridge as Mary, Frederic March as Tyrone, Bradford Dillman as Edmund and Jason Robards, Jr as Jamie. In the *New York Herald Tribune* for 9 November 1956, Walter Kerr wrote that O'Neill 'seems to be reassuring [his family's] ghosts, wherever they may be, that he knows everything awful they have done, and loves them'. But it was the source of O'Neill's new style that most exercised the critics. Brooks Atkinson in the *New York Times* thought the play was 'like a Dostoevsky novel in which Strindberg had written the dialogue', and Robert Coleman in the *Daily Mirror* saw it as 'overlong Chekhov, with a vengeful bile and too little genuine compassion'. Let us say that the play was uniquely O'Neill at his best: powerful, ugly, irresistible theatre.

The alcoholic Jamie appeared again as a character fourteen years older, and comforted in his guilt by a Junoesque farm-girl, in *A Moon for the Misbegotten*, a comic-pathetic sequel to *Long Day's Journey*. This play had its opening in Columbus, Ohio, directed by Arthur Shields of the Abbey Theatre and played only by actors of Irish extraction; but it everywhere ran into opposition from the censor. It was written in the same mode of realism, intense and obsessed, that O'Neill seems to have settled for at the end. Like his other plays, it can be wordy and repetitive, and its ideas are often banal, but it is nevertheless unexpectedly effective in the theatre, where its strong feelings provide first-rate acting material, and can emotionally entrap an audience in the agonized world of its characters.

26. Eugene O'Neill, *Long Day's Journey into Night*, New York, 1956. Directed by José Quintero. Act IV, with Florence Eldrich, Bradford Dillman (standing left), Jason Robards (standing right) and Frederic March.

15 *Realism in America: Williams and Miller*

The Glass Menagerie (1945), *Death of a Salesman* (1949)

Two American playwrights, both writing essentially in the realistic mode, have by their achievement justified the dogged American pursuit of realism. Arthur Miller and Tennessee Williams are not the Ibsen and Chekhov of the modern theatre, but the differences between their ways of seeing the world around them suggests the differences between the Norwegian and the Russian. Where Miller is more explicit, Williams is oblique. Where Miller presses home a judgment, Williams refuses even an opinion.

The dramatic world of Tennessee Williams (1914–) is crowded with the personal terrors that lie in wait for its victims. His most endearing play remains his early success *The Glass Menagerie* (1945). The setting of the play announces the soul-destroying urban environment of a southern family living in St Louis on its memories, a little like the family in *Three Sisters*. The unconventional scene design for its first production, one of translucent and transparent walls made with the help of scrim, gauze and special lighting, was not, its designer Jo Mielziner explained in his book *Designing for the Theatre*, 'trying to escape its responsibility of dealing with reality, or interpreting experience, but is actually or should be attempting to find a closer approach, a more penetrating and vivid expression of things as they are. . . Williams was writing not only a memory play but a play of influences that were not confined within the walls of a room.' However, the non-realistic framework of the play, in which the son of the family, Tom Wingfield, plays chorus to the scenes of his memory, and even the Piscator devices of expressionistically projected titles and images (dropped in the New York production without damaging the fabric of the play), scarcely disturbed the Chekhovian detail of the main action.

The reviewers agreed that *The Glass Menagerie* was a play of 'mood' and lacked dramatic action in the accepted sense. Although Louis Kronenberger in the *New York Times* of 2 April 1945 was troubled by the play's external devices ('Chekhov worked from within, as Mr Williams does not'), he went on to claim that, 'In its

27. Tennessee Williams, *The Glass Menagerie*, New York, 1945. Setting by Jo Mielziner; with Eddie Dowling and Julie Haydon.

mingled pathos and comedy, its mingled naturalistic detail and gauzy atmosphere, its preoccupation with "memory", its tissue of forlorn hopes and backward looks and languishing self-pities, *The Glass Menagerie* is more than a little Chekhovian.' The play was found by Wilella Waldorf in the *New York Post* to have a genuine poetic quality, and 'like life itself, it is deeply touching, very funny, desperately sad'. The gently sardonic humour and human understanding with which Amanda Wingfield, the mother, tries to revive the old-fashioned courtesies in order to snare a 'gentleman-caller' for her daughter, and the delicacy with which the actress Laurette Taylor conveyed her threadbare dignity as a faded belle, made her the most Chekhovian character yet seen in American drama, mixing a little of the ageing selfishness of *The Seagull*'s Mme Arkadina with the warmth and generosity of *The Cherry Orchard*'s Mme Ranevsky.

A first portrait of Williams's typical woman of sorry self-delusion had appeared in an early one-act play with the ironic title, *The Lady of Larkspur Lotion* – larkspur lotion being commonly used against lice. In the play a New Orleans prostitute tries desperately to maintain her pathetic pretensions to gentility. She is comforted by a man living in the same derelict tenement, and he gives her a glass of whisky and announces himself as 'Anton Pavlovitch Chekhov', an amusing touch not without meaning for the playwright's interests at this time. This lady appeared again in 1947 as a major character in Williams's masterpiece, *A Streetcar Named Desire*. In this unprecedented play, Blanche Dubois is another lady of doubtful morals who also feeds on her dreams. She is forced to live with her better-adjusted sister Stella in a wretched apartment in a back street of New Orleans. Blanche's delusions of grandeur and her incessant chatter cleverly convey her inability to face the truth about herself, and her rape by her brother-in-law Stanley Kowalski symbolizes how out of place are her genteel fantasies in a brutal and hostile environment.

Elia Kazan directed *Streetcar* for the Group Theatre, with Jessica Tandy as Blanche, supported by the Method actors Marlon Brando, Karl Malden and Kim Stanley. In *In Search of Theater*, Eric Bentley reported that the play seemed 'more realistic than it is', and put this effect down to Kazan's direction. In his working method, Bentley said, Kazan first sought the 'spine' of each character, comparable with Stanislavsky's 'super-objective'. Blanche's inner world, the world of her old home Belle Reve, the scene of her self-dramatization, was the lyrical reality he tried to establish, and the source of the production's style. Against the tracery of her delusions, he set the world of the brutish Kowalski, one in which Blanche could appear to be only a misfit, 'a butterfly in a jungle'. In the notebook Kazan kept during the production, he also recognized another reality in the play, one in which Blanche was 'a heightened version of an artistic intensification of all women', so that 'she should be played, should be dressed, should move like a stylized figure'. This treatment was one of poetic realism, and it was complemented by Mielziner's skeleton setting of translucent walls, with the lighting directing the audience's attention on only one part of the stage at a given moment, so creating 'space that is limited but has the illusion of infinity'.

After these successes, Williams continued to create further archetypes of spiritual loneliness, if with a little less compassion.

28. Tennessee Williams, *A Streetcar Named Desire*, New York, 1947. Directed by Elia Kazan, setting by Jo Mielziner. Scene viii, with Jessica Tandy, Marlon Brando and Kim Stanley.

The Rose Tattoo (1951) was a comedy outstanding for its ironic ingredients. It portrays a Sicilian community living on the Gulf Coast, and there one Serafina Delle Rose has outrageously dedicated her life to her love for her dead husband. But Serafina is another self-deceiver, and when she is trapped by her own exuberant sexuality, she incongruously consoles herself with a passing truck-driver. Mixing lyricism and coarseness, pathos and ridicule, Williams achieves an extraordinary and precarious balance. The play takes a step from Chekhov's to O'Casey's kind of realism, and the result is almost a black comedy. *Cat on a Hot Tin Roof*, directed by Elia Kazan in 1955, depicts a whole family of self-deceivers; this time they are more wealthy, and living in a mansion on a Mississippi plantation. The father is convinced that he is not dying from cancer; his homosexual son has taken to drink; the son's young wife believes that she can still attract him. Gaiety is on the surface; all beneath lies despair. In such images there is pain and shock, repressed passion and violence. Williams had increasingly super-charged the common experience of life to create an almost grotesque world of human beings living on the constant edge of crisis. Accordingly, he developed a heightened dialogue which had its roots in real speech, but which was twice as expressive. And no play-wright in America had demonstrated a greater sense of the stage, a keener eye for human incongruity and conflict.

It is interesting that, like any obsessed realist, Williams must return again and again to the scene of his obsession. In 1978, he dared to offer a dramatic epitome of his past sources of inspiration in the significantly named *Vieux Carré*, and actually used an auto-biographical narrator, like Tom Wingfield of *The Glass Menagerie*, to speak for him. Vieux Carré is the Old Quarter of New Orleans, and there the author revisits his ghosts. These include Jane, a genteel Blanche Dubois who has succumbed to temptation and taken a lover; Nightingale, a consumptive homosexual painter; and a Mrs Wire, a grim rooming-house keeper who is nevertheless quite vulnerable beneath her fierce exterior. In New York, these reitera-tions were less welcome, but in London at the Piccadilly Theatre, the production by Keith Hack made a point of the nostalgia itself in the classic Tennessee Williams way, with the familiar skeletal frame setting moving on a revolve to the accompaniment of repeating

musical motifs. Why this winging back to the past of thirty years
ago? Writing in the *Daily Mail* of 16 August 1978, Jack Tinker
suggested that as 'our modern poet for the lonely, the outcast and the
isolated', Williams was cleansing our sins by his compassion and
his humour. And in this play, the playwright has demonstrated his
ability to smile and not shout at his victims, so that a fitting distance
from total realism is achieved, and the author's artistic detachment
is finally complete.

Arthur Miller (1915–   ) attracted critical attention in
1947 when he presented a strong social drama in the Ibsen
manner, *All My Sons*, which tells of a pillar of the community, a
businessman who sells defective aircraft to the Army during the
war. This play was appropriately played by Group actors and
directed by Elia Kazan. Kazan also directed Miller's best-known

29. Arthur Miller, *Death of a Salesman*, New York, 1949. Directed
by Elia Kazan, setting by Jo Mielziner. L to r: Mildred Dunnock,
Lee J. Cobb, Arthur Kennedy, Cameron Mitchell.

play, *Death of a Salesman* in 1949, with Mielziner as designer. This play has assumed the role of being the representative American play of the mid-century. The intensity of its realistic dialogue reduced a moralistic tendency and element of social criticism in the writing, and enhanced its 'tragic' properties, especially in the projection of the central character Willy Loman, whose failure touched a nerve among audiences everywhere. The American idiom of the character was fully realized by the Group actor Lee J. Cobb. The play's style sufficiently obscured its darker purpose, and suggested that Miller had shifted his allegiance slightly away from Ibsen and closer to Chekhov.

Loman is the salesman who has a salesman's competitive philosophy: he needs to believe in his own value as 'vital to New England' even when he knows he is not. So he drags his family down with him in his self-deceit and particularly destroys the illusions of his son Biff, whom he idealizes and who idealizes him. The episodic structure of the play builds a contrast between Willy's romantic images of the past and the hard reality of the present, and this contrast was emphasized by Mielziner's careful changes in lighting from a sunlit green to more sombre tones. In his notebook for the play, Kazan recorded his decision that the viewpoint in the scenes from the past was always Willy's, as if these were his daydreams and the play itself were his confession. In fact, Miller's first title for the play was *The Inside of His Head*. The representation of Willy's interior drives and compulsions, set against his anxieties and defensive fictions, encouraged Kazan to look for a hidden motive behind every line, and carry into the flat prose of the dialogue a range of tones, inflections and rhythms that brought the play intensely alive on the stage.

Death of a Salesman was universally acclaimed as a 'suburban tragedy', and in the distinguished Introduction to his *Collected Plays* of 1958, Miller reviewed his position and 'commitment' as a dramatist. The 'poetry' of a play, he argued, had nothing to do with its realism or non-realism, but with the 'organic necessity of its parts'. He believed that Ibsen not merely showed what happened, but also accounted for the process and development of events. Ibsen documented the past as heavily as he did because an understanding of the roots of the present was

necessary for any 'higher consciousness'. So Miller explained that
in writing *Death of a Salesman*, he did not set out to write a
tragedy, or to measure Willy's stature by any Greek or Elizabethan
standards for a tragic hero. In the modern age, social rank did not
determine the tragic experience; rather, 'the common man is as apt a
subject for tragedy in its highest sense as kings were'. What
mattered was the conscious experience of the central character in his
pride and dignity. Willy Loman had broken the law of success in
society, a law without which life was insupportable, and the
audience's reaction was not to be 'What happens next and why?'
so much as 'Oh, God, of course!' The structure of the play was
determined by 'what was needed to draw up [Willy's] memories like
a mass of tangled roots without end or beginning'. Miller did not use
so centrifugal a form for a play again, unless for *After the Fall* in 1964,
because it could not be grafted on to a character whose mind it did
not reflect. In any case, it takes the talent of a director with a bent
for the psychological like Elia Kazan to make a unity of a play based
on the complexities of mind of one character.

Arthur Miller is an unrepentant moralist as neither Ibsen nor
Chekhov were. He continued to pursue an ideal of overtly purposeful,
social drama, especially in *The Crucible* (1953) dealing with the
Salem witch trials in colonial New England, a play of protest
intended to reflect the political persecution of Senator Joseph
McCarthy's Un-American Activities Committee after the war.
Although the hero of the play, John Proctor, is drawn into the common catastrophe through no fault of his own, the drama is set out in
colours that are morally too black and white, too comforting and
facile, to achieve its intended import in maintaining its audience.
Since we know Proctor to be in the right, we feel righteous ourselves. *A View from the Bridge* (1955) more successfully investigates
the tragic possibilities of the Italian immigrant code of loyalty in
Brooklyn, a code which traps the half-articulate dock-worker Eddie
Carbone. Less surely, a chorus-figure in the image of a local lawyer
is undramatically called upon to underline the meaning behind the
action. Like Williams, Miller has worked with, and departed from,
the accepted mode of realism, but he is wedded to the belief that
the role of the playwright is to project ideas upon an audience.
Unfortunately, he does not share Ibsen's further dimension of poetic
mysticism.

It is fitting to name one or two more American playwrights of the 1950s whose attraction was due especially to their exploration of realism. William Inge (1913–73) was encouraged in his playwriting by Tennessee Williams, and in technique these two have much in common. A native of mid-west America, Inge wrote with careful detail in the Chekhovian manner of the kind of people he knew from Kansas and Missouri in the 1930s and 1940s. His second play, *Come Back, Little Sheba*, was produced by the Theatre Guild in New York in 1950 with Daniel Mann as director; by the standards of Broadway it was only a modest success, running for less than six months. It takes a simple situation of an uneasy marriage, and focuses hard on the two characters of the husband and wife. 'Doc' Delaney, played by Sidney Blackman, is a reformed alcoholic, and his agony in struggling to keep his dignity in a home run by his easy-going wife Lola, played by Shirley Booth, steadily reaches a terrifying crisis as the two face a common future of despair.

Half the reviewers approved; some were violently repelled. John Chapman in the *New York Daily News* of 16 February 1950 thought the play 'part Chekhov, part Arthur Miller and part the divine gospel of Alcoholics Anonymous'. Yet this play remained Inge's most convincing treatment of human need and mutual dependence. Lola's recurrent dream about her lost dog Sheba gently and unobtrusively symbolizes her lost youth and good looks, the couple's lost baby and everybody's lost hopes from the past. The ending is lyrically Chekhovian as Lola finally decides that Sheba is never coming back, while Doc silently sips his fruit juice.

Inge wrote of his guiding principles as a playwright in his Foreword to a collection of four of his plays published in 1958. He said he had no wish to write a play that primarily told a story: 'I regard a play as a composition rather than a story, as a distillation of life rather than a narration of it', and he described *Come Back, Little Sheba* as 'a fabric of life' in which the characters were 'species of the environment'. He turned then, he said, to fill a larger canvas and 'to write plays of an over-all texture that made fuller use of the stage as a medium'. So he avoided the kind of intense scene like that in which Doc drunkenly threatens Lola's life, and instead sought 'breadth' and not 'depth': 'I like to keep several stories going at once, and to keep as much of the playing area on stage as alive as possible.

I use one piece of action to comment on another, not to distract from it.' Inge was here prescribing a formula for Chekhovian realism.

The play in which he put his new plan to the test was *Picnic* (1953). This brings a handsome drifter, Hal Carter, to a small town in Kansas, where his flaunted virility upsets the lives of a group of frustrated women. The setting is the porch and yard of a shabby house, where Hal attracts the prettiest girl, and then leaves her flat. This cold ending was changed for the Theatre Guild's production in New York, directed by Joshua Logan and designed by Mielziner, and the girl followed the man she loved at the final curtain. Walter Kerr, writing in the *New York Herald Tribune* on 20 February, thought Logan's direction too emphatic for the 'fragile summer-sunset mood' of the play, and we might well think that Chekhov had also made his exit when the substituted ending abruptly exploded the understated action in what had gone before. It is especially ironic that Inge had written in an article about *Picnic* that a play should be compared with 'a journey in which every moment should be as interesting as the destination'.

He considered that his next play, *Bus Stop* (1955) had even less of a story ('*Bus Stop*, I suppose, has less real story than any play that ever survived on Broadway'). The pattern and texture were the

30. William Inge, *Picnic*, Theatre Guild, New York, 1953. Directed by Joshua Logan, setting by Jo Mielziner.

merit of the play, and he sought dramatic values, he said, in a relative way, seeing a character in comparison with another. In this play, for example, 'the cowboy's eagerness, awkwardness, and naïveté in seeking love were interesting only when seen by comparison, in the same setting, with the amorality of Cherie, the depravity of the professor, the casual earthiness of Grace and Carl, the innocence of the schoolgirl Elma, and the defeat of his buddy Virgil'. Yet was the throwing together of characters, however well compared, at a bus stop or at a picnic, enough to justify a play? Inge's plays, with their flat mid-western speech and straightforward depiction of character, demonstrate his compassion for the banal lives and spiritual poverty of the people he chooses, but offer no more than sentimental solutions to their problems.

There is another field in which realism came into its own in the 1950s. The photographic realism natural to the television medium, the small 'psychological' detail of expression and gesture of the actor in close-up, the domestic framework best suited to a popular home medium, the reduced human and social content appropriate to television drama, encouraged a new group of playwrights to emerge in the early years of the medium's development. This group included the naturalistic writers Tad Mosel, Reginald Rose, Rod Serling and Paddy Chayefsky (1923 –   ). Chayefsky practised typically understated writing, and his 1953 television portrait of *Marty*, a lonely, unattractive man, with the unattractive job of butcher, from the Bronx, is of a man too shy to get a 'date' until he meets an unattractive girl as shy as himself. Chayefsky had nicely reduced the dramatic scale of his play for the new medium, and *Marty* proved to be a moving story of common human need in the large city. He repeated the same limited kind of success with *Middle of the Night* (televised 1954, staged 1956). This is a tender account of an unpretentious Jewish widower who wishes to marry a girl young enough to be his daughter in the face of his family's objections. In these early plays for television, Chayefsky wrote in a light and humorous, but deliberately minor, key about very ordinary people, and the greater scale necessary for the stage eluded him when he turned to larger themes.

The catalogue of American playwrights of the 1960s and 1970s who in some degree continue to use realistic speech and manners, if in a symbolic framework, could be extended from Edward Albee (1928–   ) with the educated vocal pyrotechnics of *Who's Afraid of Virginia Woolf?* (1962), to Chicago's David Mamet (1947–   ) with his precise ear for the popular rhythms and humour of urban mid-western speech, as in *American Buffalo* (1977). That so many American playwrights have demonstrated the impact of the Chekhovian manner on their work should not be surprising, since the influence of Stanislavsky and The Method is all-pervasive in the actors' schools in the United States. And in turn the development of realistic acting was nourished by the myriad fragmentary details with which a character is given life in the Chekhovian way. The best American plays acquired techniques of honesty, objectivity and restraint, and aimed for the realistic standard with a pattern of careful discords, the surface in conflict with the reality beneath, one attitude set against another, a character divided against himself. The incongruous juxtaposing of truth with appearances, of what a person says with what he does, resulted in a comic undercutting and ironic balancing on the stage, with a consequent distancing of the audience which was itself evaluative. This kind of comic realism, whether it is called 'dark' or 'black', is pathetic at one moment, bitter at the next, and colours a social drama with a quite unsentimental ambivalence. It is this ambivalence which has proved attractive to a sceptical modern age in which 'the centre cannot hold', to quote Yeats's painful diagnosis of the malaise of modern times.

16 New realism in Britain: 1956 to the present

Look Back in Anger (1956), *Roots* (1959), *Saved* (1965)
   In his lectures at Princeton in 1944, Granville-Barker suggested that there were two ways of playwriting, the explicit and the implicit, and that these radically affected the ways of acting. He chose Chekhov for his example:

> Unless the actress of Madame Ranevsky brings to her
> performance not only all she is directed to say and do, but
> something besides that she must pervasively and expressive-
> ly *be* (and the same thing will be true and truer of acting in
> the later plays of that both 'explicit' and 'implicit' dramatist
> Ibsen), there will be left in the place the character should
> fill nothing but a very large hole (*The Use of the Drama*,
> p.45).

The best tradition of realism in Britain since Shaw has certainly
been implicit in feeling, indeed, at times so underplayed as to be
scarcely felt on the surface at all. The new realism in Britain after
the Second World War had far more explicit work to do.

In an abrasive article in 1957 entitled 'They Call It Cricket',
John Osborne wrote forthrightly, 'I want to make people feel, to
give them lessons in feeling.' He spoke as a new playwright for a
new generation, and his choice of words was exact. The feeling was
loosely polemical, socialistic and evangelical, but the requirement to
give 'lessons' in feeling has curiously stretched the forms of realism.
With few exceptions, like the early plays of Harold Pinter, which do
not properly belong in a discussion on realism, Granville-Barker's
wish for implicit playwriting is forgotten, and in the total perspec-
tive of European and American realism, the British contribution
may not count for much. Typically working from practice and not
theory, it has produced no major dramatist and offered no new
dramatic example to the rest of the world. However, it has resulted
in the flourishing of a home-grown drama more plentiful and more
challenging than anything seen for years.

Between the wars, the London theatre had declined into a
mediocrity of quasi-realistic drama. Now an eruption of new writing was caused by young dramatists who appeared to return
to the roots of realism without so much as a nod to theatrical
tradition. Their work was variously identified as 'kitchen sink
drama', 'dustbin drama', 'angry theatre', 'committed theatre',
and so on. It was variously explained by the aftermath of war and
disillusion with the first Labour Party majority in Parliament, by the
spirit of 1956, the year of Suez and the Hungarian uprising, by the
spirit of rebellion against a feudal social structure in Britain. But it
was a particular rebellion against the conventional, middle-class

fare of the London theatre, especially the verse drama of T. S.
Eliot and Christopher Fry. The new drama might be parochial, but
it would be a vigorous prose drama of ideas, an attempt to breach
the wall which, in Arthur Miller's words, 'seals the British theatre
from life'. It would strike hard at one of Britain's cherished
cultural institutions, and if this meant forsaking the drawing-room
for the kitchen, so be it.

Britain's minor dramatic renaissance derived from no favour-
able school of acting as in America, no leader of dramatic form and
style as in Germany, no public debate about the direction of contemporary theatre as in France, but from the work of virtually one
man. The actor and director George Devine (1910–66) provided
a home for new playwrights by founding the English Stage Company

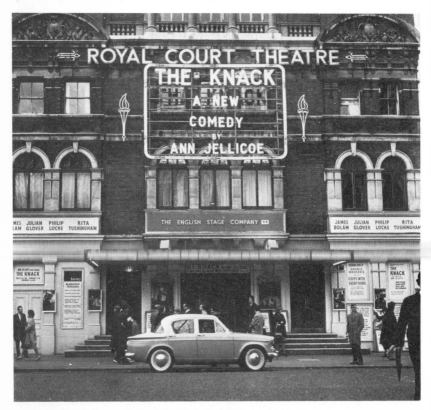

31. Royal Court Theatre, London, in 1962.

at the Royal Court Theatre in 1956. Although the Royal Court was some way from the West End, was hardly a comfortable theatre and seated only 614, it had been the very place where Bernard Shaw had achieved recognition under the Vedrenne-Barker management of 1904—7. Within a few weeks it again became the focus of theatrical attention, and its drama the subject of public discussion — London was not used to this. Within six years the company had presented nearly 100 plays, of which 64 were by new authors, many of whom were now launched on a playwriting career. The movement had a spokesman in Kenneth Tynan, the polemical critic of *The Observer*, and a lively forum in the periodical *Encore*. Celebrated actors of the old school had to make the decision whether to resist or assist the new drama. But it was essentially a playwright's theatre, defiantly working-class in orientation, attacking the comfortable craftsmanship and dull thinking of the established theatre. Unskilled in the ways of the professional stage, the new writers at least had youth on their side, each one individually mapping his course by trial and error.

Devine's declared policy was to promote a 'writers' theatre' both by encouraging new dramatists and by urging novelists and poets to try their hand at playwriting. He remained open-minded towards the increasing flood of scripts that arrived on his desk, holding playreadings without costume and one-night productions without décor as a way of deciding which plays should graduate to the main stage. Devine may have been wrong not to establish a permanent acting company to achieve a consistent style of performance; he may have been wrong not to work up a repertory system to nurse a radical play into acceptance with the public; but the English Stage Company, and Joan Littlewood's Theatre Workshop in the East End, together made London a centre for experimental theatre virtually overnight.

The subjects of the plays struck audiences as new — often the life of the urban or rural working-class, a group which had traditionally been used only as a pool of comic characters. (In 1968, the Royal Court rediscovered D. H. Lawrence's Nottingham plays, *A Collier's Friday Night* of 1906, *The Daughter-in-Law* of 1912 and *The Widowing of Mrs Holroyd* of 1914, which had been unacceptable fifty years before.) With this unaccustomed social group came a new range of regional speech and a refreshing vitality in the dialogue: *Look Back in Anger* is set insolently in Birmingham, Shelagh Delaney drew upon Lancashire, Alun Owen upon Liverpool, and so on. Accordingly, the well-furnished elegance of the middle-class stage gave place to kitchens and attics, with all their sordid paraphernalia of cooking stoves and ironing boards and beds. Nevertheless, it is surprising that so many of the new plays, even those by novelists like Angus Wilson and Muriel Spark, fell back upon the structure of the well-made play, aiming for the conventional emotional climax and often achieving only a sentimental resolution. The greatest weakness was the failure of a working-class drama to recruit a working-class audience, a failure of which Arnold Wesker was particularly conscious. And when innovators like John Osborne turned to historical subjects (*Luther*, 1961) and middle-class themes (*West of Suez*, 1971), it was symptomatic of a fatal new respectability.

32. John Osborne, *Look Back in Anger*, Royal Court Theatre, London, 1956, with Kenneth Haigh as Jimmy Porter, Alan Bates as Cliff and Mary Ure as Alison.

The explosion of the new realism was first felt when *Look Back in Anger* by John Osborne (1929–   ) was produced at the Royal Court in 1956, directed by Tony Richardson. There was little sense to be had from some of the notices that the play would be a watershed in British theatre. A leader in *The Times* on 26 May considered the play's central character, Jimmy Porter, to be 'a thoroughly cross young man', and then excused him by adding that 'most young men, in every age, are probably much alike', even daring to predict that 'it is likelier that the real tone of our age will be found much closer to that of a century ago'. Its drama critic had also been rather cool on 9 May: 'This first play has passages of good violent writing, but its total gesture is altogether inadequate', going on to explain:

> The piece consists largely of angry tirades. The hero regards himself, and clearly is regarded by the author, as the spokesman for the younger post-war generation who looks round at the world and finds nothing right with it.

This comment probably expressed the common view of the play, but Kenneth Tynan's advocacy in *The Observer* on 13 May swept aside all opposition. Was Jimmy Porter to be considered no more than a young pup?

> What with his flair for introspection, his gift for ribald parody, his excoriating candour, his contempt for 'phoneyness', his weakness for soliloquy and his desperate conviction that the time is out of joint, Jimmy Porter is the completest young pup since Hamlet, Prince of Denmark . . . Jimmy is simply and abundantly alive; that rarest of dramatic phenomena, the act of original creation, has taken place . . . I doubt if I could love anyone who did not wish to see 'Look Back in Anger'. It is the best young play of its decade.

Tynan had never written with more wit, pointing out that the issue was not one of good theatrical taste: 'The Porters of our time deplore the tyranny of good taste.' And Harold Hobson of *The Sunday Times* capped the idea of the play's commitment to a new moral cause by quoting a line by Jimmy's wife Alison in act II, when she cries, 'I want a little peace': 'It is peace that she gets in the end', wrote Hobson, 'as Raskolnikov gets it when he ceases to maintain himself innocent.'

As a play, *Look Back in Anger* is deficient in some respects. Its characters are short on the kind of motivation a naturalistic drama calls for, and Osborne hardly attends to the others on the stage with Jimmy. Like much of Osborne, it is not written with economy, a point made by Hobson when he complained that 'the inexhaustible outpouring of vicious self-pity comes near to wearying the audience's patience', and it ends with a sentimentally convenient reconciliation between Jimmy and Alison. But the play completely justified the efforts of the English Stage Company to discover a new playwright with something to say. Jimmy Porter had the 'genuine modern accent', the 'authentic new tone' of the 1950s. Yet no word was spoken of any need to develop a new technique of drama to match it. Brecht and Beckett had come and gone as if they had never been, and 'kitchen sink' drama seemed to mean that the British theatre was wedded to naturalism.

The importance of *Look Back in Anger* was greater than its value as good drama. It was the company's third production, and the early box-office success of this play subsidized the production of many others, only a few of which were profitable. All the plays of John Arden, for example, consistently lost money, even though *Serjeant Musgrave's Dance* (1959) has since been widely played in colleges and prescribed for study in schools. The success of *Look Back* also taught a lesson, that notoriety was an important part of avant-garde theatre. Osborne's play had directly provoked a conflict in its audience between the social classes and between the generations, all in one formula: older members of the Royal Court audience were confronted by a low-class young malcontent who had dared to marry a well bred girl and drag her down by his spiritual malaise. After this, insulting the audience would become one of the tactics of the new movement.

Only remnants of Osborne's aggressive realism were left in his next play, *The Entertainer* (1957). Yet Archie Rice, its central figure, was again provocatively ambiguous. A pathetic, second-rate music-hall comic, he had evaded the truth about his life by practising a sardonic wit which he carried home from his unattractive work. The Berliner Ensemble had visited London in 1956, giving playgoers their first taste of Brecht on the stage, and now Osborne wrapped his play in a quasi-Brechtian frame. The theatre itself became a replica of the dying British music-hall, and its decadent mixture of old-fashioned patriotism and sleazy sex was made outrageously to symbolize the state of the country. This was a brilliant stroke of theatre, against which the public image of the clown could be modified by the private image of Archie's broken home life, and for Osborne it opened up possibilities of dramatic satire less dependent on the forms of realism.

Because of Osborne's stylistic virtuosity, he often leaves his audience in two minds. We admire Kenneth Haigh's Jimmy Porter and Laurence Oliver's Archie Rice, while intensely disliking their power over us. The shapeless, uncertainly humorous *tour de force* which some think Osborne's finest piece of realistic writing was *Inadmissible Evidence* (1964). This play is a virtual monologue, for its centrepiece is a shabby lawyer named Bill Maitland, who, when he is not talking to others, is talking to himself. He is in process of losing his wife, his mistress, his daughter and his clients; even the various marital cases he takes on all reflect his own marriage, a point theatrically underlined by having each client played by the same actress. So he roams his seedy office, in Bernard Levin's phrase, 'on symbolic trial for the crime of existing'. The stream of words flows on two levels, public and private, sometimes inseparably, and if the inability to communicate is a theme of the post-war drama, it is here executed as a form of dialogue. As a realistic portrait of a middle-aged man in despair at the direction his life has taken, the play is a small masterpiece of sustained monologue, and no finer example of this volubility can be found than the tirade Maitland levels at his daughter of seventeen and her generation: 'Fifteen hundred unfalteringly fluent words delivered in one great rush like coal sliding off a tip-up lorry', is Levin's description, 'yet never relaxing their grip on our imagination.' But as Maitland speaks, the girl stands in silence judging him and his generation, and it is her silence which is more eloquent than all his words and makes the most profound moral comment in the play.

Yet, we may ask, does all this make a play which truly speaks to its audience, or is it a psychological study for the merely curious, a photographic record of a human failure fit only to be filed away? Maitland's troubles touch a common sore from time to time, but in his self-pity is he sufficiently representative of the human condition, in its self-indulgence is the play our common property? Perhaps an essential dimension of good realism is missing. The point is further made when we question the audience's attitude to Nicol Williamson's performance as Maitland in 1964 and again in the revival of 1978, generally acclaimed as one of the great performances of the modern British theatre. Do we share the anguish of the character or wonder at the actor's constant vocal variety, indulging the character or the actor? The lack of distance, the uncertain comedy, of *Inadmissible Evidence* betrays the brilliant writing. Realism is never enough in itself: it must always be artfully unreal.

The early plays of John Arden (1930–), especially *The Waters of Babylon* (1957) and *Live Like Pigs* (1958), seemed to place him among the new realists, and although he refused to fall into the didactic trap, from the beginning his work appeared to bristle with naturalistic purpose. *Live Like Pigs* was his most naturalistic play, and presents a cosy suburban family, the Jacksons, who have their lives violently disrupted by their neighbours, the Sawneys, a family of gipsies housed by the local council. Neither family is attractive, and Arden sets up a provocative situation without condemning one side or the other, or pressing home some lesson on social conformity or the dangers of the welfare state. Audiences were unprepared for the responsibility of thinking for themselves. Then in 1959 Arden showed his true colours. His inclination towards dramatic dialectic is clear throughout *Serjeant Musgrave's Dance*, a play whose position on the subject of pacificism is meticulously ambiguous, and whose form is invigorated by Brechtian devices of historicizing and distancing. Arden called this play 'an unhistorical parable' and 'a realistic, but not a naturalistic, play', and he aimed at a sharper objectivity in the scenes by inserting realistic detail into stylized action. Arden soon discovered the limitations of verisimilitude, and his break with naturalism will be discussed in volume 3.

Although Arnold Wesker (1932–) flirted with nonrealistic structural devices, he has been the most truly naturalistic of the first Royal Court group of new playwrights. He is a thesis dramatist who regularly risks the pitfalls of the preacher, but his early trilogy of plays devoted to the political mores of the working-class was as daring an endeavour as anything in this period. To support the central argument, 'If you don't care, you'll die', the first of the three plays, *Chicken Soup with Barley* (1958) dramatized the saga of a Jewish family living in the East End of London from just before the Second World War, a time of clashes in the streets between right and left wing factions, to a time of disillusion after the war. The second play, *Roots* (1959), possibly represents Wesker's finest work. It is delightfully oblique in its didacticism, with its message conveyed more organically within the realism of the play. The self-education of a young woman, Beatie Bryant, in rural Norfolk in a sense becomes the education of Wesker's audience. In keeping with the viewpoint of a single character, *Roots* in less rambling than *Chicken Soup*, and succeeds in promoting a thesis while depicting the authentically real. It invites experience before demanding belief, and as we reject Beatie's glib boyfriend and the soulless indifference of her family, we accept her conversion. The third play, *I'm Talking about Jerusalem* (1960), transports two members of the original family to a 'new Jerusalem' also in Norfolk, but Wesker is less successful in excluding his personal feelings and in exploiting the ironic mode of *Roots*.

Roots was first produced at the Belgrade Theatre, Coventry, the home of many discoveries at this time. It was transferred to the Royal Court and finally crowned by a transfer to the Duke of York's Theatre in the West End. It was directed by John Dexter, and its design by Jocelyn Herbert was significantly authentic and evocative. Alan Brien described it for *The Spectator* of 10 July 1959:

> The setting is a farm labourer's kitchen — scruffily cosy,
> meagrely cluttered, with hand-me-down furniture, zigzag
> linoleum, gaudy wallpaper, a clock and a radio both
> designed like jerry-built Greek temples, and (of course) the
> over-stuffed sink.

This was truly 'rural kitchen sink', an accurate background for an ugly and stupid home life among 'the tepid, torpid farm animals' who constitute Beatie's family. The mother, 'with cottage-loaf figure and Yorkshire-pudding face', was played by Gwen Nelson for shallow good nature and 'the sometimes terrifying savagery of the stupid'.

This setting was the springboard for an idea — as *The Times* expressed it, 'the unpopular (but surely undeniable?) truth that many people close to the earth lead brainless, pointless, ignoble lives, and that if these are our roots, the sooner we sever all connexion the better'. The play's title is nicely ironic, and Beatie, played exuberantly by Joan Plowright, is used to show the family what might be. Yet the trick of the play is that she has been living with Ronnie Kahn of *Chicken Soup*, so that all her criticisms of rural life are

33. Arnold Wesker, *Roots*, Royal Court Theatre, 1959. Directed by John Dexter, setting by Jocelyn Herbert, with Joan Plowright as Beatie Bryant.

apparently his, thus keeping him ironically at bay and making Beatie herself amusingly acceptable. But there's more than the parrot in Beatie when she breaks into a wild dance in act II. As a gramophone spins out the farandole from *L'Arlésienne,*

> the daughter begins to prance around in her bare feet, eyes closed, fingertips widespread, in a parody of a ballet. Mother jogs her old bones and mutters indulgently, 'She's like a young lamb'. Curtain to the second act of *Roots.*

Wasn't this enough sentiment to make your hair curl? asked Alan Brien. On the contrary, he found it 'the most touching and true incident' he had seen 'in eighteen months of theatre-going'. In *The Sunday Times* of 5 July, Harold Hobson found the episode 'frankly incredible; sensible people like Beatie don't do such things', and 'nothing in the play's naturalism has prepared us for this leap into Dionysiac frenzy'; but he concluded that 'it is at this moment that one recognizes unmistakably that Mr Wesker is a dramatist'. When at the end it is revealed that Beatie's intellectual lover Ronnie really is a phoney, having failed to turn up at the family gathering, Brien concluded that her joyous dance is balanced by the stage picture at the final curtain, 'when the family chorus, grunting and snuffling, jostle round the trough, happily transformed to beasts again'. Ronnie has left her defenceless, but as she stands apart and alone it is exquisitely suggested that, in spite of Ronnie, the family, her roots, she has suddenly had her own insight into the nature of things.

The audience has an insight too. Yet it is not surprising that the play had a mixed reception in Coventry, London and New York. The Norfolk dialect made a totally unfamiliar sound, which *The Times* thought a formidable disadvantage, and a stageful of authentically dull-witted characters made for a rather inarticulate dialogue. The danger of boring an audience with bores is ever-present in naturalistic drama, and uneventful lives are a doubtful basis for stage action. But *Roots* was nevertheless in the true naturalistic tradition, the most faithful play to have appeared about the British working-class without sentimentalizing them as noble victims.

In the years after 1956, there was some confusion about which new playwrights belonged naturally to the 'kitchen sink' school. Like Arden's, the early plays of Harold Pinter (1930–   ) were at first assumed to be of the realistic movement because of his choice of lower-class backgrounds and his gift of reproducing the idiom of Cockney speech. Pinter, however, had in fact made Samuel Beckett his starting-point, and is better considered as a symbolist. And within ten years, a second group of vigorous young writers had followed the first, although less tied to the forms of realism. Many of these began by writing realistically, only to be seduced into experimenting with expressionistic and absurdist and other effects as Ionesco, Beckett and Brecht made themselves felt in the British theatre. Edward Bond (1935 –   ) stands out as one who has passed from a vividly realistic picture of society at its lowest level in *Saved* (1965) to more extravagant and unreal images of violence and fear as in his reworking of Shakespeare's material in *Lear* (1971).

When *Saved* was produced at the Royal Court, directed by William Gaskill, it called down upon its author's head charges of sadism and obscenity because of a central scene in which a baby in a perambulator is smeared with its own excrement and then stoned to death by a gang of teenage thugs. The correspondent to *The Times* thought this was the ugliest scene he had seen on

34. Edward Bond, *Saved*, Royal Court Theatre, London, 1965.
Directed by William Gaskill. Scene vi.

any stage, and damned the play as 'a blockish naturalistic piece'
interested only in 'a systematic degradation of the human animal':

> [Mr Bond] has written a work which will supply valuable
> ammunition to those who attack modern drama as half-
> baked, gratuitously violent, and squalid. Why on earth did
> the theatre accept it?... One can no longer take cover
> behind the phrase 'bad taste' in the face of such material.
> But one has a right to demand what purpose it fulfils.

The law at first allowed the play to be presented under 'theatre
club' conditions, then the Lord Chamberlain found legal reasons
for prohibiting even this kind of performance. The direct result
of this action was the abolition by Parliament of all stage censorship
in 1967. These events made an important public issue of the degree
of realism the stage could admit, but distracted attention from the
play's merits. In a public discussion held at the theatre on 14 November 1965, Mary McCarthy supported the play for what she called
its 'remarkable delicacy' in depicting the truth. In a letter to *The
Observer*, Laurence Olivier also came to the defence of the play by
pointing out that Bond had placed his act of violence in the first
half of his play, as Shakespeare had in *Macbeth* and *Julius Caesar*,
and implied that Bond thereby turned the focus of interest on the
thoughtful aftermath of the sensational action.

Much of the difficulty for the audience is that *Saved* is too
accurately naturalistic in conception and execution. Bond has
managed to write a dialogue for a class of nearly inarticulate
persons – indeed, *The Times* considered it 'slavishly literal'. And the
human situation is perfectly well imaginable. The baby is conceived
without being wanted. Because it is not wanted, it cries all the time,
until the ignorant mother drugs it with aspirin. In this condition,
the baby is left alone in its pram and becomes the centre of interest
to a gang of boys. With only good intentions, the boys talk to it, but
when it does not respond they commit the terrible act of stoning. In
his introduction to *The New Theatre of Europe* (1970), Martin Esslin
summarized the matter thus: 'So, the horrible, brutal physical act
of the killing of the baby is the objectification, the concretization of
a moral problem: the problem of the unloved child produced by
people of subnormal intelligence who are unable to exercise self-

control or responsibility.' Esslin went on to suggest the larger analogies of this action, citing as instances the SS man who killed a Jew because he could not imagine his victim's feelings, and the bomber pilot who could drop his load of bombs because he was unable to see his human target for himself. And in his 'Author's Note' to the play, Bond himself has argued that the stoning was 'a typical English understatement': 'Compared to the "strategic" bombing of German towns it is a negligible atrocity, compared to the cultural and emotional deprivation of most of our children its consequences are insignificant.'

Bond went even further. In his note he claimed that the play was a comedy:

> *Saved* is almost irresponsibly optimistic. Len, the chief
> character, is naturally good, in spite of his upbringing and
> environment, and he remains good in spite of the pressures
> of the play... The play ends in a silent social stalemate,
> but if the spectator thinks this is pessimistic that is because
> he has not learned to clutch at straws. Clutching at straws
> is the only realistic thing to do.

In all the savagery of the play, the youth Len has stayed loyal to the baby's mother. The extremity of the situation is justified as a way of measuring how slim is the fraction of hope that Bond finds in so desperate a life. When at the end of the play Len decides to stay and mend a chair on the line, 'Fetch me 'ammer', that is the gleam of hope in a hopeless situation. The play touches Bond's recurrent theme, that innocence is always open to corruption by the callousness of others. But it roused the angry feeling it did because it placed violence and evil in a wholly realistic setting. No character stood apart and talked about violence and evil; the play simply represented it. The low dialogue of the play was not written to discuss the people who spoke it; it merely served to present them. Esslin reported that in Vienna a version in German came to life only when the low speech was translated into the equivalent German vernacular, and added that if the play was to work in America, it would have to be translated into the equivalent American verna- cular. This is realism indeed, with the aesthetic gap between the world of the stage and the world of the audience reduced to a minimum. When Bond moved on to write in a more surrealistic way, his images were not so painful.

This is a sample of realistic British playwrights who have emerged since the war. Some, like David Mercer (1928–80) and David Storey (1933–   ), have dramatized human behaviour almost exclusively in a realistic vein. Others have extended the convention of realism in serio-comic ways. *A Day in the Life of Joe Egg* (1967) by Peter Nichols (1927–   ) is a black comedy about the lives of the parents of a spastic child, but played in the manner of a game into which the audience is drawn. *Entertaining Mr Sloane* (1964) by Joe Orton (1933–67) deals in a black humour which pushes a realistic situation almost into the grotesque; his later plays go all the way into farce.

The upsurge of original British playwriting which began in 1956 was not a movement like that of naturalism in Europe at the end of the nineteenth century. It did not base itself on any consistent body of theory — traditionally suspect in Britain in any case. From the beginning, its form of realism was uncertain, and the audience could never be sure whether the next product would be a masterpiece or a muddle. But the new realism was a strong force for artistic liberation, and the British theatre witnessed an unusual number of new plays written without restriction of subject, form or language. A corps of new actors cultivated regional manners and accents to meet the need, and did so as carefully as they had previously prepared themselves to play Shakespeare. An increase in the number of provincial theatres has been a further, unexpected by-product. It is a direct result of the new spirit in the theatre that a climate for experiment exists in post-war London which in scope rivals that of pre-war Paris.

17 *Realistic theatre: retrospectively*

The realistic impulse, the desire to reproduce on the stage a piece of life faithfully, has been persistent over the last hundred years, even when realism as a technique has varied constantly in purpose and kind. The aggressive naturalism with which a Zola sets out to drill his audience into seeing what it cannot see for itself can give way to the gently oblique impressionism by which a Chekhov tries to woo his audience towards a fresh perception. As a convention, realism may be practised rigorously from start to finish of a performance, so that some Strindbergian illusion may be hypnotically complete, or it can be touched in like an occasional illustration to make a tall tale from Ireland ring true. A realistic play may explore the human psyche in the manner of an Ibsen or an O'Neill, to the point where it must concede the unreal devices of expressionism or symbolism if it is to probe any further, or its ideas may prompt a debate in the mind of the audience, to the point where only the introduction of a Shavian dialectic can satisfy the appetite created. In spite of all these variations, or perhaps because of them, the ability to depict a realistic scene seems to be an indispensable tool in the hands of the modern dramatist and his actors. And they will inevitably return to the fathers of modern realism to learn its secrets.

The momentous accomplishment of the great master realists, Ibsen, Strindberg and Chekhov, casts a giant shadow over all those plays which seek a new direction for drama in the twentieth century. Their work stands as the absolute measure for most modern attempts at realistic playwriting. Some could have wished for a little more of Ibsen in Arthur Miller or John Osborne, a little more of Strindberg in Eugene O'Neill, a little more of Chekhov in Bernard Shaw or Tennessee Williams. And as we look back at the total contribution of the realistic movement, it is also clear that the principles and standards of realistic acting as established by

Stanislavsky and the Moscow Art Theatre in the first place have been immensely serviceable to all dramatic media, including film and television, and today can hardly be ignored by an actor in training. Realism has placed important new aesthetic demands upon all parties to the play, playwright, actor, director and spectator.

Major plays in the realistic manner have been written since the war. It has been asked, indeed, whether a new wave is not merely a tired old wave still rippling. Naturalism is properly recognized as the great movement of the nineteenth century in the novel and drama, and the one from which all significant departures in the twentieth had to be made. Nevertheless, some realistic action, however brief and hidden, is usually the basis for a dramatic conception, or the source of essential contrast with any unreal activity on the stage. Poor Tom is Lear's fantastic *alter ego*, and at the same time the true picture of beggary. Even non-realistic theatre, such as the great medieval religious cycles or the high poetic drama of the Elizabethans, was good because it kept one foot on the ground, and from time to time slipped in a realistic character or incident to remind the popular audience of the earthy reality.

However, reaction against the theatre of psychological realism and of ordinary speech and behaviour was relentless throughout the twentieth century. We shall see how the forces against it themselves divided into symbolism and expressionism. On the one hand, the strong personal feeling which prompted a more lyrical and imaginative stage after Ibsen and Maeterlinck resulted in the more symbolic representation of life as a dream, a state of mind, a heightened perception – a development which readily threw up other, more surrealistic or even absurdist, stage images. On the other hand, the social and political arguments which underpinned the best naturalistic drama continued as powerfully rational and satirical dramatic statements, taking up a cause where a realistic play of ideas had left it, and sometimes emerging as a poetic vision that was expressionistic in form, and appealing as much to the reason as to the emotions.

The two succeeding books attempt to separate and trace these lines of development in the pattern of modern drama – the symbolist and the expressionist, the Artaudian and the Brechtian.

Table of events in the theatre

1 **Realism and naturalism**
2 Symbolism, surrealism and the absurd
3 Expressionism and epic theatre

[The entries in **bold type** are the subject of this volume]

Legend: w = written, p = produced, f = formed, d = died

World events	Writers, artists and events in the theatre	Plays and productions
1851		
Louis Napoleon president of France	'Opera and Drama' w Wagner	
Great Exhibition, London	Ibsen directing in Bergen and Christiana (to 1862)	
	limelight in use	
1859		
'Origin of Species' w Darwin		
1861		
Italy unified		
American Civil War (to 1865)		
1865		
Lincoln assassinated		'Tristan and Isolde' w Wagner
		'Society' w Robertson
1866		
	Saxe-Meiningen company f Georg II	'Brand' p Ibsen
1867		
Dominion of Canada		'Peer Gynt' p Ibsen
'Das Kapital' w Marx		**'Caste' w Robertson**
Baudelaire d		

World events	Writers, artists and events in the theatre	Plays and productions
1870		
Franco-Prussian War (to 1871)	Dumas père d	
Dickens d		
1871		
Germany unified	'Purpose of the Opera' w Wagner	
1872		
	'The Birth of Tragedy' w Nietzsche	
1873		
		'Thérèse Raquin' p Zola
1874		
	Saxe-Meiningen company on tour	
1876		
telephone invented	Bayreuth theatre built	'The Ring cycle' p Wagner
1877		
gramophone invented		**'Pillars of Society' w Ibsen**
1879		
		'A Doll's House' w Ibsen
		Büchner's 'Woyzeck' published
1880		
George Eliot, Flaubert d	**'Naturalism in the Theatre' w Zola** electric light in the theatre	**'Pillars of Society ['Quicksands'] in London**
1881		
Dostoevsky d		**'Ghosts' w Ibsen**
1883		
	Deutsches Theater, Berlin f Wagner d	**'Ghosts' p Stockholm 'The Wild Duck' w Ibsen**
1887		
	Théâtre-Libre, Paris f Antoine	**'The Father' w Strindberg**

World events	Writers, artists and events in the theatre	Plays and productions
1888		
	Dagmar Theatre, Copenhagen f Strindberg	**'Power of Darkness' w Tolstoy 'Miss Julie' w Strindberg**
1889		
Browning d	**Freie Bühne, Berlin f Brahm**	**'A Doll's House' p London and New York**
1890		
Van Gogh d	**Freie Volksbühne, Berlin f Wille** Boucicault d	**'Ghosts' p Paris 'Hedda Gabler' W Ibsen** 'The Intruder', 'The Blind' w Maeterlinck
1891		
Melville, Rimbaud d	**Independent Theatre Company, London f Grein 'Quintessence of Ibsen- ism' w Shaw**	**'Ghosts' p London** 'Spring's Awakening' w Wedekind
1892		
Tennyson d		**'The Weavers' w Hauptmann 'Widowers' Houses' w Shaw** 'Countess Cathleen' w Yeats
1893		
Maupassant, Tchaikowsky d	Théâtre de l'Oeuvre f Lugné-Poe	**'Mrs Warren's Profession' w Shaw** 'Pelléas and Mélisande' w Maeterlinck
1894		
	Brahm at Deutsches Theater	**'Arms and the Man' w Shaw** 'Land of Heart's Desire' w Yeats
1895		
first films made	'La Mise-en-scène du drame Wagnérian' w Appia	**'A Doll's House' in America**

World events	Writers, artists and events in the theatre	Plays and productions
		'Earth Spirit' w Wedekind
1896		
Verlaine d	'The Treasure of the Humble' w Maeterlinck	'Salomé' p Lugné-Poe 'Ubu roi' p Jarry **'The Seagull' in St Petersburg**
1897		
Brahms d	**Moscow Art Theatre f Stanislavsky and Danchenko**	
1898		**'The Seagull' p MAT**
Mallarmé d		'To Damascus' w Strindberg
1899		
Boer War (to 1902)	'Die Musik und die Inszenierung' w Appia **Irish Literary Theatre f Yeats and Lady Gregory**	'When We Dead Awaken' w Ibsen **'Uncle Vanya' w Chekhov**
1900		
Nietzsche d	Wilde d	'To Damascus' p Stockholm
1901		
Commonwealth of Australia Queen Victoria d Freud's 'Interpretation of Dreams'		'Easter' w Strindberg **'Three Sisters' w Chekhov**
1902		
	Kleines Theater, Berlin f Reinhardt **Zola d**	'A Dream Play' w Strindberg **'The Lower Depths' w Gorky** 'Danton's Death' p Berlin
1903		
Wright brothers' flight		**'Shadow of the Glen' w Synge**
1904		
Entente Cordiale	**Abbey Theatre, Dublin f**	**'The Cherry Orchard' w Chekhov**

World events	Writers, artists and events in the theatre	Plays and productions
Russo-Japanese War (to 1905)	**English Stage Society at Court Theatre (Vedrenne and Barker)** **Chekhov d**	**'Riders to the Sea' w Synge** 'On Baile's Strand' w Yeats
1905		
	'The Art of the Theatre' w Craig Reinhardt at Deutsches Theater Meyerhold at MAT Studio	**'Mrs Warren's Profession' p New York** **'Man and Superman' w Shaw** Reinhardt's 'Midsummer Night's Dream', Berlin
1906		
Cézanne d	Appia meets Dalcroze Meyerhold in St Petersburg Reinhardt f Kammers-pielhaus **Ibsen d**	'Partage de midi' w Claudel 'Spring's Awakening' p Reinhardt 'Hedda Gabler' p Meyer-hold
1907		
Dominion of New Zealand	Intima Teatern, Stockholm f Strindberg Jarry d	'Ghost Sonata' w Strindberg **'Playboy of the Western World' w Synge** 'The Life of Man' w Andreyev 'Murderer, the Hope of Women' w Kokoschka
1908		
	'L'umorismo' w Pirandello	'The Blue Bird' w Maeterlinck
1909		
Ballets Russes in Paris	'The Mask' ed. Craig (to 1929) **Synge d**	
1910		
Union of South Africa King Edward VII d	'The Tragic Theatre' w Yeats **Tolstoy d**	'Oedipus Rex' p Reinhardt 'Dom Juan' p Meyer-hold
1911		
first Post-Impressionist		'The Miracle'

World events	Writers, artists and events in the theatre	Plays and productions
exhibition		p Reinhardt **Synge's 'Playboy'** **p New York**
1912 second Post-Impressionist exhibition Titanic disaster	Debussy's 'L'Après-midi d'un faune' p Nijinsky **Brahm d** **Strindberg d**	'Hamlet' p Craig in Moscow Shakespeare at the Savoy p Barker 'Theatre of the Soul' w Evreinov 'The Beggar' w Sorge
1913 Freud's 'Interpretation of Dreams' trans. into English 'Sons and Lovers' w Lawrence	Vieux Colombier f Copeau Stravinsky's 'Le Sacre du printemps' p Nijinsky	'The Mask and the Face' w Chiarelli 'Danton's Death' and 'Woyzeck' p Munich 'Burghers of Calais' w Kaiser
1914 First World War (to 1918)	Kamerny Theatre, Moscow f Taïrov MAT Third Studio f Vakhtangov	Barker's 'Midsummer Night's Dream' at the Savoy
1915 Lusitania torpedoed	**Provincetown Players,** **Washington Square** **Players f New York**	'Patricide' w Bronnen
1916 Easter Rebellion, Dublin Henry James d	Dada exhibition, Zürich 'Theatre Arts' published New York	**'Heartbreak House'** **w Shaw** 'At the Hawk's Well' w Yeats 'Right You Are' w Pirandello 'From Morn to Midnight' w Kaiser
1917 America enters the War Russian Revolution Jung's 'Psychology of the	Copeau in New York (to 1919) Reinhardt's 'Das junge Deutschland'	'The Breasts of Tiresias' w Apollinaire 'Parade' w Cocteau Kaiser's 'Gas' trilogy

World events	Writers, artists and events in the theatre	Plays and productions
Unconscious' trans into English		
1918		
Armistice signed	Wedekind d	**O'Neill's one-act**
Debussy d		**plays of the sea**
		'Baal' w Brecht
1919		
'Cabinet of Dr Caligari' (film) made	Reinhardt f Grosses Schauspielhaus, Berlin	'The Transformation' w Toller
Renoir d	**Theatre Guild, New York f**	
	The Bauhaus, Weimar f Gropius	
1920		
League of Nations f	State Theatre, Moscow f Meyerhold	'The Dybbuk' p Vakhtangov
	Salzburg Festival f Reinhardt and Hofmannsthal	'The Emperor Jones' w O'Neill
	Théâtre National Populaire f	'Beggar's Opera' at the Lyric, Hammersmith
1921		
Irish Free State f	Atelier f Dullin (to 1938)	'The Wedding on the Eiffel Tower'
	MacGowan's 'Theatre of Tomorrow'	w Cocteau
		'Six Characters in Search of an Author'
		w Pirandello
		'R.U.R.' w Karel Čapek
		'Masses and Man' w Toller
1922		
Mussolini in power in Italy	**MAT visits Paris and**	'Henry IV' w Pirandello
Irish Civil War	**Berlin**	'The Hairy Ape'
radio broadcasting begins	**American Laboratory**	w O'Neill
'Ulysses' w Joyce	**Theatre f**	'The Magnanimous
'The Waste Land' w Eliot	'Continental Stagecraft' w Macgowan and Jones	Cuckold' p Meyerhold
	Vakhtangov d	'Turandot' p Vakhtangov
1923		
	Schlemmer's Bauhaus Theatre (to 1929)	Triadic Ballet p Schlemmer
		'The Adding Machine'

World events	Writers, artists and events in the theatre	Plays and productions
		w Rice
	MAT visits New York	'Knock' p Jouvet
	Bernhardt d	
1924		
Stalin in power in Russia	**'My Life in Art' w**	**'Juno and the Pay-**
'The Magic Mountain' w	**Stanislavsky**	**cock' w O'Casey**
Mann	Copeau's school in Burgundy	'The Infernal Machine'
Puccini d	First surrealist manifesto	w Cocteau
		'Desire under the
		Elms' w O'Neill
	Provincetown experi-	Piscator's 'Rowdy Red
	mental season, New	Revue'
	York	
	Piscator at the Volksbühne	
1925		
	Pirandello f Teatro d'Arte,	Berg's opera 'Wozzeck'
	Rome	**'Hamlet' in modern**
		dress
1926		
British General Strike	Théâtre Alfred Jarry f	**'Plough and the**
'Metropolis' (film) made	Artaud and Vitrac	**Stars' w O'Casey**
		'Great God Brown' w
		O'Neill
		'A Man's a Man' w
		Brecht
		'Inspector General' p
		Meyerhold
1927		
Pavlov's Conditioned	Piscator national Polit-	'The Spurt of Blood' w
Reflexes trans into	Theater	Artaud
English	Isadora Duncan d	'Hurrah, We Live!' w
		Toller p Piscator
1928		'Threepenny Opera'
Thomas Hardy d	O'Casey leaves Ireland	w Brecht
	Appia d	'The Silver Tassie' w
		O'Casey
		'The Good Soldier
		Schweik' p Piscator
1929		
Wall Street crash: world	**Group Theatre, New**	**'Street Scene' w Rice**
economic depression	**York f**	'Amphitryon 38' w
first 'talkie'	Religious Drama Society f	Giraudoux

World events	Writers, artists and events in the theatre	Plays and productions
	'The Political Theatre' w Piscator Diaghilev d	'The Bedbug' w Mayakovsky
1930 D. H. Lawrence d	Baty at Théâtre Mont-parnasse	Rise and Fall of the City of Mahagonny' w Brecht 'The Bathhouse' w Mayakovsky
1931	Lorca's La Barraca f Madrid Saint-Denis f La Compagnie des Quinze (to 1935) Piscator's Drama Workshop f New York	'Noah' w Obey 'Atlas-Hôtel' w Salacrou 'Mourning Becomes Electra' w O'Neill
1932	first manifesto of the Theatre of Cruelty Okhlopkov at the Realistic Theatre, Moscow	
1933 Hitler in power in Germany Roosevelt president in America (to 1945) *1934*	second manifesto of the Theatre of Cruelty	'Blood Wedding' w Lorca 'Within the Gates' w O'Casey
	Jouvet at Théâtre Athenée Pitoëff at the Théâtre aux Mathurins	**'The Children's Hour' w Hellman** 'Yerma' w Lorca
1935 Federal Theatre Project in America (to 1939)	Theatre of Cruelty f Artaud	**'Waiting for Lefty' w Odets** 'The Trojan War Will Not Take Place' w Giraudoux 'Murder in the Cathedral' w Eliot
1936 Spanish Civil War first public television	**Stanislavsky's 'An Actor Prepares' trans. into English** Pirandello, Lorca d	'The House of Bernarda Alba' w Lorca 'School for Wives' p Jouvet

World events	Writers, artists and events in the theatre	Plays and productions
1937		**'Golden Boy' w Odets**
		'Electra' w Giraudoux
1938		
Germany annexes Austria	Artaud's 'Theatre and Its	'Les Parents terribles' w
Munich agreement	Double'	Cocteau
	Brecht's 'Street Scene'	'Our Town' w Wilder
	Stanislavsky d	
1939		
Second World War	**Yeats**, Toller, Pitoëff d	**'The Little Foxes' w**
(to 1945)		**Hellman**
		'Galileo', 'Mother
		Courage' w Brecht
1940		
Paris occupied, Battle of	Barrault at the Comédie-	'Good Woman of
Britain	Française	Setzuan' w Brecht
Churchill prime minister	Meyerhold, Lugné-Poe d	'Purple Dust' w O'Casey
1941		
Germany and Russia	Brecht in America	'Mother Courage'
at war	(to 1947)	p Zürich
Pearl Harbor: America		
enters the War		
Joyce d		
1942		
	'The Myth of Sisyphus'	'The Flies' w Sartre
	w Camus	'Skin of Our Teeth'
		w Wilder
		'Red Roses for Me' w
		O'Casey
1943	**Antoine, Danchenko**,	'Antigone' w Anouilh
	Reinhardt d	
1944		
D-Day landing in	German and Austrian	**'Glass Menagerie'**
Normandy	theatres closed	**w Williams**
	Giraudoux d	'Caligula' w Camus
		'Huis clos' w Sartre
1945		
first atomic bomb	Littlewood's Theatre	Giraudoux's 'Madwoman
United Nations f	Workshop f	of Chaillot' p Jouvet

World events	Writers, artists and events in the theatre	Plays and productions
Labour in power in Britain	Kaiser, Jessner d	'Caucasian Chalk Circle' w Brecht
1946		
	Compagnie Renaud-Barrault f (to 1956)	**O'Neill's 'Iceman Cometh'p**
	Hauptmann d	'Men without Shadows w Sartre
1947		
	Actors' Studio f New York	**'Streetcar Named Desire' w Williams**
	The Living Theatre f Beck and Malina	Barrault p Kafka's 'The Trial'
		'The Maids' w Genêt p Jouvet
		'Galileo' p in America
1948		
Israel proclaimed Czechoslovakia communist	Brecht's 'Little Organon for the Theatre'	'Les Mains sales' w Sartre
	Artaud d	Barrault p Claudel's 'Partage de midi'
1949		
	Ionesco f Collège de 'Pataphysique	**'Death of a Salesman' w Miller**
	Brecht, Weigel f Berliner Ensemble	'The Cocktail Party' w Eliot
	Maeterlinck, Copeau, Dullin d	'Cock-a-Doodle Dandy' w O'Casey
1950		
Korean War (to 1953)	Piscator back in Germany	**'Come Back, Little Sheba' w Inge**
McCarthy hearings in America (to 1954)	**Shaw.** Taïrov d	'The Bald Soprano' w Ionesco
1951		
Festival of Britain	Vilar at the Théâtre National Populaire (to 1963)	**'The Rose Tattoo' w Williams**
	Jouvet d	
1952		
H-bomb tested	'Saint-Genêt' w Sartre	'Waiting for Godot' w Beckett
	Cage at Black Mountain College	'The Parody' w Adamov

World events	Writers, artists and events in the theatre	Plays and productions
1953		
East German uprising	Shakespeare Festival of	**'The Crucible' w**
Stalin d	Canada	**Miller**
	O'Neill d	'Professor Taranne' w
		Adamov
		'Camino Real w Williams
1954		
Algerian Civil War (to	'Theatre Problems' w	'Amédée' w Ionesco
1962)	Dürrenmatt	
Matisse d	Berliner Ensemble at	
	first Paris festival	
1955		
	Littlewood at Stratford,	**'View from the**
	East London	**Bridge' w Miller**
	Claudel d	'Ping-pong' w Adamov
		'War and Peace' p
		Piscator
1956		
Hungarian uprising	**English Stage Com-**	**O'Neill's 'Long Day's**
Suez Canal crisis	**pany at Royal Court**	**Journey' p**
	Theatre f Devine	**'Look Back in Anger'**
	Berliner Ensemble in	**w Osborne**
	London	'The Visit' w Dürrenmatt
	Brecht d	'The Balcony' w Genêt
1957		
Treaty of Rome establishes		'Endgame' w Beckett
European Economic		'The Blacks' w Genêt
Community		'The Entertainer' w
first Russian space flight		Osborne
Sibelius d		
1958		
De Gaulle president of		'Picnic on the Battle-
France (to 1969)		field' w Arrabal
Berlin airlift		'The Birthday Party' w
		Pinter
		'The Fire Raisers' w
		Frisch
1959		
	Polish Lab Theatre f	**'Roots' w Wesker**
	Grotowski	'The Zoo Story' w Albee
	San Francisco Mime	'Serjeant Musgrave's

World events	Writers, artists and events in the theatre	Plays and productions
	Troupe f Davis '18 Happenings' p Kaprow	Dance' w Arden
1960		
	Peter Hall p Royal Shake- speare Company (to 1968) Camus d	'The American Dream' w Albee 'The Happy Haven' w Arden
1961		
American forces in Vietnam Berlin Wall erected	Bread and Puppet Theatre, New York La Mama Experimental Theatre Club, New York	'Happy Days' w Beckett 'Andorra' w Frisch
1962		
Cuban missile crisis Lincoln Center for the Performing Arts opened New York (completed 1969)	Ionesco's 'Notes and Counter Notes' Esslin's 'Theatre of the Absurd'	'Exit the King' w Ionesco **'Who's Afraid of Virginia Woolf?' w Albee** 'The Physicists' w Dürrenmatt Brook's 'King Lear' for RSC
1963		
President Kennedy assassinated	National Theatre f London Brook's Theatre of Cruelty season The Open Theatre f New York Tzara, Cocteau, **Odets d**	'The Brigg' p Malina 'The Workhouse Donkey' w Arden Littlewood's 'Oh, What a Lovely War' Hochhuth's 'Represen- tative' p Piscator
1964		
	Living Theatre in Europe **O'Casey d**	'Marat/Sade' w Weiss Grotowski's 'Akropolis'
1965		
	second Berliner Ensemble visit to London Eliot d	'Marat/Sade' p Brook **'Saved' w Bond** 'Frankenstein' p Beck
1966		
	Kirby's 'Happenings' Craig, Breton, Piscator d	'A Delicate Balance' w Albee 'America Hurrah' w van Itallie p Chaikin

World events	Writers, artists and events in the theatre	Plays and productions
		'Insulting the Audience' w Handke
1967		
	The Performance Group f New York **Rice d**	'Rosencrantz and Guildenstern Are Dead' w Stoppard 'The Architect and the Emperor of Assyria' w Arrabal
1968		
Paris riots stage censorship lifted in Britain	'The Empty Space' w Brook 'Towards a Poor Theatre' w Grotowski 'Notes towards a Definition of Documentary Theatre' w Weiss	'Paradise Now' p Beck 'Dionysus in 69' p Schechner 'Kaspar' w Handke
1969		
American moon landing		Grotowski's 'The Constant Prince' 'Christie in Love' w Brenton
1970		
	International Centre for Theatre Research in Paris	Brook's 'Midsummer Night's Dream' 'AC/DC' w Heathcote Williams **'Home' w Storey**
1971	Brook's Festival at Persepolis Vilar, Adamov d	'Old Times' w Pinter 'Lear' w Bond
1972		
	Weigel d	'Jumpers' w Stoppard
1973		
Britain joins the Common Market	Hall at National Theatre	'Nightwalk' p Chaikin 'Bingo' w Bond 'Brassneck' w Brenton and Hare
1974		
		'Travesties' w Stoppard

World events	Writers, artists and events in the theatre	Plays and productions
1975		
Watergate scandal in Washington	Wilder d	**'Norman Conquests' w Ayckbourn** 'Comedians' w Griffiths **'American Buffalo' w Mamet**
1976		
Vietnam war ends American Bicentennial	National Theatre opens on the South Bank	'The Ik' p Brook 'Weapons of Happiness' w Brenton
1978		
		'The Woman' w Bond
1979		
		'Betrayal' w Pinter

Bibliography

This is a comprehensive list of works, chiefly in English, covering the subject of realism and naturalism in modern drama.

MODERN DRAMA: SURVEYS AND GENERAL CRITICISM

Abel, Lionel, *Metatheatre*, 1963
Bentley, Eric, *The Dramatic Event*, 1957
    — *In Search of Theater*, 1963
    — *The Life of the Drama*, 1964
    — *The Modern Theatre (The Playwright as Thinker)* 1946
    — *Theatre of War*, 1970
    — *What Is Theatre?*, 1957
    — ed., *The Theory of the Modern Stage*, 1948
Bermel, Albert, *Contradictory Characters: An Interpretation of the Modern Theatre*, 1973
Bogard, Travis, and Oliver, William I., eds., *Modern Drama: Essays in Criticism*, 1965
Bradbury, Malcolm and McFarlane, James, eds., *Modernism 1890–1930*, 1978
Bradby, David and McCormick, John, *People's Theatre*, 1978.
Brockett, Oscar G., *History of the Theatre*, 3rd edn, 1977
    — *Perspectives on Contemporary Theatre*, 1971
    — *The Theatre: An Introduction*, 1966
    — and Findlay, Robert R., *Century of Innovation: A History of European and American Theatre and Drama since 1870*, 1973
Brown, John Mason, *The Modern Theatre in Revolt*, 1929
Brustein, Robert, *The Culture Watch: Essays on Theatre and Society, 1969–1974*, 1975
    — *Seasons of Discontent: Dramatic Opinions, 1959–1965*, 1965
    — *The Theatre of Revolt*, 1962
    — *The Third Theatre*, 1969
Carter, Huntly, *The New Spirit in the European Theatre, 1914–1924*, 1926
Cheney, Sheldon, *The Art Theatre*, 1925
    — *The New Movement in the Theatre*, 1914
    — *The Theatre: Three Thousand Years of Drama, Acting and Stagecraft*, 1929
Chiari, Joseph, *Landmarks of Contemporary Drama*, 1965
Clark, Barrett H., *European Theories of the Drama*, revised Henry Popkin, 1965

Cohn, Ruby, *Currents in Contemporary Drama*, 1969
Cole, Toby, ed., *Playwrights on Playwriting*, 1960
  — and Chinoy, Helen Krich, eds., *Actors on Acting*, 1949
  — *Directors on Directing*, 1963
Corrigan, Robert W., *The Theatre in Search of a Fix*, 1973
Dickinson, Thomas H., ed., *The Theatre in a Changing Europe*, 1937
Driver, Tom Faw, *Romantic Quest and Modern Query: A History of the
     Modern Theatre*, 1970
Fergusson, Francis, *The Idea of a Theater*, 1949
Flanagan, Hallie, *Shifting Scenes of the Modern European Theatre*, 1928
Freedley, George and Reeves, John A., *A History of the Theatre*, 3rd edn,
     1968
Gascoigne, Bamber, *Twentieth Century Drama*, 1962
Gaskell, Ronald, *Drama and Reality*, 1972
Gassner, John, *Form and Idea in the Modern Theatre*, 1956
  — *Theatre at the Crossroads*, 1960
  — *The Theatre in Our Times*, 1954
  — and Allen, Ralph Gilmore, *Theatre and Drama in the Making*, vol. 2,
     1964
  — and Quinn, Edmund, eds., *The Reader's Encyclopedia of World
     Drama*, 1969
Gilman, Richard, *The Making of Modern Drama*, 1974
Goldberg, Roselee, *Performance: Live Art 1909 to the Present*, 1979
Gorelik, Mordecai, *New Theatres for Old*, 1962
Grossvogel, David I., *The Blasphemers: The Theatre of Brecht, Ionesco,
     Beckett and Genêt*, 1965
Guthke, Karl S., *Modern Tragicomedy: An Investigation into the Nature
     of the Genre*, 1966
Hainaux, René, ed., *Stage Design throughout the World since 1935*, 1956
  — *Stage Design throughout the World since 1950*, 1964
  — *Stage Design throughout the World, 1970—1975*, 1976
Heilman, R.B., *The Iceman, the Arsonist, and the Troubled Agent: Tragedy
     and Melodrama on the Modern Stage*, 1973
Isaacs, Edith J. R., ed., *Theatre: Essays on the Arts of the Theatre*, 1927
Kennedy, Andrew, *Six Dramatists in Search of a Language*, 1975
Kienzle, Siegfried, *Modern World Theatre: A Guide to Productions in Europe
     and the United States since 1945*, trans. A. Henderson, 1970
Kitchin, Laurence, *Drama in the Sixties: Form and Interpretation*, 1966
Krutch, Joseph Wood, *'Modernism' in Modern Drama*, 1953
Lagner, Lawrence, *The Magic Curtain*, 1951
  — *The Play's the Thing*, 1960
Lewis, Allan, *The Contemporary Theatre*, 1962
Lumley, Frederick, *Trends in Twentieth Century Drama*, 1960
Macgowan Kenneth, and Jones, Robert Edmond, *Continental Stagecraft*,
     1922

Marshall, Norman, *The Producer and the Play*, 1957

Matlaw, Myron, *Modern World Drama: An Encyclopedia*, 1972

Miller, Anna Irene, *The Independent Theatre in Europe, 1887 to the Present*, 1931

Melchinger, Siegfried, *The Concise Encyclopedia of Modern Drama*, 1964

Moussinac, Léon, *The New Movement in the Theatre: A Survey of Recent Developments in Europe and America*, 1931

Nagler, A. M., *A Source Book in Theatrical History*, 1959

Nicoll, Allardyce, *The Development of the Theatre*, 4th edn, 1958

Oppenheimer, George, *A Passionate Playgoer*, 1958

Schwarz, Alfred, *From Büchner to Beckett: Dramatic Theory and the Modes of Tragic Drama*, 1978

Simonson, Lee, *The Stage Is Set*, 1932

Styan, J. L., *The Dark Comedy: The Development of Modern Tragic Comedy*, 2nd edn, 1968

Vardac, A. Nicholas, *Stage to Screen: Theatrical Method from Garrick to Griffith*, 1969

Vinson, James, ed., *Contemporary Dramatists*, 1977

Wellek, René, *A History of Modern Criticism: The Later Nineteenth Century*, 1965

Wellwarth, George, *The Theatre of Protest and Paradox*, 1964

Whitaker, Thomas R., *Fields of Play in Modern Drama*, 1977

Whiting, John, *The Art of the Dramatist*, 1970

Williams, Raymond, *Drama from Ibsen to Brecht*, 1968
— *Modern Tragedy*, 1966

Young, Stark, *The Flower in Drama: A Book of Papers on the Theatre*, 1923
— *Glamour: Essays on the Art of the Theatre*, 1925
— *Immortal Shadows: A Book of Dramatic Criticism*, 1948
— *The Theatre*, 1927
— *Theatre Practice*, 1926

REALISM IN FRANCE: THE NINETEENTH CENTURY

Becker, George J., *Documents of Modern Literary Realism*, 1963

The Drama Review: TDR 42: 'Naturalism Revisited', winter 1968

Dumas, Alexandre, *fils*, 'Au lecteur' in *Théâtre complet*, vol. I, 1868
— *A Propos de la Dame aux camélias*, 1867

Hobson, Harold, *French Theatre since 1830*, 1979

Hugo, Victor, Preface to *Cromwell*, 1827
— Preface to *Hernani*, 1830

Lemaître, Jules, *Impressions de théâtre*, 11 vols., 1888—1920
— *Selections*, ed. Russell Scott, 1930
— *Theatrical Impressions*, trans. Frederic Whyte, 1924

Matthews, Brander, *French Dramatists of the Nineteenth Century*, 1905

Sarcey, Francisque, *Quarante ans de théâtre*, 8 vols., 1900—2

Stanton, Stephen S., Introduction to *Camille and Other Plays*, 1957

Weinberg, Bernard, *French Realism: The Critical Reaction, 1830–1870,* 1937

Émile Zola
— *The Experimental Novel, and Other Essays,* trans. B. M. Sherman, 1893
— *Le Naturalisme au théâtre,* 1881
— *Nos Auteurs dramatiques,* 1881
— Preface to *Thérèse Raquin,* 1873, trans. Kathleen Boutall in E. R. Bentley, ed., *From the Modern Repertoire,* 1956

André Antoine
— *Memories of the Théâtre-Libre,* trans. Marvin A. Carlson, 1964

Clark, Barrett H., *Contemporary French Dramatists,* 1916
— *Four Plays of the Free Theatre* (preface by Brieux), 1915
Moore, George, *Impressions and Opinions,* 1891
Waxman, S. M., *Antoine and the Théâtre-Libre,* 1926

REALISM IN SCANDINAVIA
Beyer, Harald, *A History of Norwegian Literature,* 1956
Blankner, Frederika, ed., *The History of the Scandinavian Literatures,* 1938
Jorgenson, Theodore, *History of Norwegian Literature,* 1933
Lagerkvist, Pär, *Modern Theatre,* trans. Thomas R. Buckman, 1961
Marker, Frederick J. and Lise-Lone, *The Scandinavian Theatre: A Short History,* 1975
Topsöe-Jensen, H. G., *Scandinavian Literature from Brandes to Our Day,* 1939

Henrik Ibsen
— *Collected Works,* trans. William Archer, 12 vols., 1906–12 (vol. XII, *From Ibsen's Workshop,* trans. A. G. Chater, 1912)
trans. James Walter McFarlane, 8 vols., 1960–
trans. Michael Meyer, 16 vols., 1960–
— *The Correspondence,* trans. John Nilsen Laurvik and Mary Morison, 1905
— *Letters and Speeches,* ed. Evert Sprinchorn, 1964
— *Speeches and New Letters,* trans. Arne Kildal, 1910
Bradbrook, Muriel C., *Ibsen the Norwegian,* 1948
Brandes, Georg, *Eminent Authors of the Nineteenth Century: Literary Portraits,* trans. Rasmus B. Anderson, 1886
Downs, Brian W., *Ibsen: The Intellectual Background,* 1946
— *A Study of Six Plays by Ibsen,* 1960
Egan, Michael, ed., *Ibsen: The Critical Heritage,* 1972
Fjelde, Rolf, ed., *Ibsen: A Collection of Critical Essays,* 1965
Flores, Angel, ed., *Ibsen: A Marxist Analysis,* 1937

Franc, Miriam Alice, *Ibsen in England,* 1919
Gosse, Edmund, *Ibsen,* 1907
Gray, Ronald, *Ibsen — a Dissenting View,* 1977
Jaeger, Henrik, *Henrik Ibsen,* 1890
Knight, G. Wilson, *Henrik Ibsen,* 1962
Koht, Halvan, *The Life of Ibsen,* 2 vols., 1931
Lavrin, Janko, *Ibsen: An Approach,* 1950
Lucas, F. L., *Ibsen and Strindberg,* 1962
MacFall, Haldane, *Ibsen,* 1907
McFarlane, James W., *Ibsen and the Temper of Norwegian Literature,* 1960
Meyer, Michael, *Ibsen: A Biography,* 1967
Nordau, Max, *Degeneration,* 1895
Northam, John, *Ibsen: A Critical Study,* 1973
— *Ibsen's Dramatic Method,* 1953
Robins, Elizabeth, *Ibsen and the Actress,* 1928
Rose, Henry, *Henrik Ibsen: Poet, Mystic and Moralist,* 1913
Shaw, George Bernard, *The Quintessence of Ibsenism,* 1891
Tennant, P D. F., *Ibsen's Dramatic Technique,* 1948
Valency, Maurice, *The Flower and the Castle: An Introduction to Modern Drama,* 1963
Weigand, Hermann J., *The Modern Ibsen,* 1925
Yeats, W. B., *Plays and Controversies,* 1923
Zucker, Adolph E., *Ibsen, the Master Builder,* 1929

August Strindberg
— *Plays,* trans. Edwin Björkman, *et al.,* 7 vols., 1912–13
— *Plays,* trans. Edith and Warner Oland, 4 vols., 1913–14
— *Plays,* trans. Horace B. Samuel, 1914
— *The Plays,* trans. Walter Johnson, 1955–
— *Three Plays,* trans. Peter Watts, 1958
— *Miss Julie and Other Plays,* trans. Max Faber, *et al,* 1960
— *Seven Plays,* trans. Arvid Paulson, 1960
— *The Chamber Plays,* trans. Evert Sprinchorn, 1962
— *Twelve Plays,* trans. Elizabeth Sprigge, 1963
— *The Plays,* trans. Michael Meyer, 1964–
— *Eight Expressionist Plays,* trans. Arvid Paulson, 1972
— *Getting Married,* trans. Mary Sandbach, 1972

— *Letters to Harriet Bosse,* trans. Arvid Paulson, 1959
— *Inferno,* trans. Claud Field, 1912 and Mary Sandbach, 1962
— *Notes to Members of the Intimate Theatre* and *Open Letters to the Intimate Theatre,* in Sprinchorn, above
— *Open Letters to the Intimate Theatre,* trans. Walter Johnson, 1966

Bulman, Joan, *Strindberg and Shakespeare,* 1933
Campbell, G. A., *Strindberg,* 1933

Collis, John S., *Marriage and Genius: Strindberg and Tolstoy*, 1963
Dahlström, Carl E. W. L., *Strindberg's Dramatic Expressionism*, 1930
Gustafson, Alrik, *A History of Swedish Literature*, 1961
Johnson, Walter, *Strindberg and the Historical Drama*, 1963
Klaf, Franklin S., *Strindberg: The Origin of Psychology in Modern Drama*, 1963
Lamm, Martin, *August Strindberg*, trans. Harry G. Carlson, 1971
 — 'Strindberg and the Theatre', trans. Thomas R. Buckman, 1961
Lucas, F. L., *Ibsen and Strindberg*, 1962
MacGill, Vivian J., *August Strindberg, the Bedeviled Viking*, 1930
Madsen, Borge G., *Strindberg's Naturalistic Theatre: Its Relation to French Naturalism*, 1962
Mortensen, Brita M. E., and Downs, Brian W., *Strindberg: An Introduction to His Life and Works*, 1949
Ollén, Gunnar, *August Strindberg*, trans. Peter Tirner, 1972
Palmblad, Harry V. E., *Strindberg's Conception of History*, 1927
Reinert, Otto, ed., *Strindberg: A Collection of Critical Essays*, 1971
Sprigge, Elizabeth, *The Strange Life of August Strindberg*, 1949
Steene, Birgitta, *The Greatest Fire: A Study of August Strindberg*, 1973
Strindberg (formerly Uhl), Frida, *Marriage with Genius*, 1937
Swerling, Anthony, *Strindberg's Impact in France, 1920—1960*, 1971
Le Théâtre dans le monde, vol. ii, no. 1, 1962
Uddgren, G., *Strindberg the Man*, 1920
Valency, Maurice J., *The Flower and the Castle* [with special reference to Ibsen and Strindberg], 1967

REALISM IN GERMANY
Brahm, Otto, *Kritische Schriften über Drama und Theater*, 1913
Grube, Max, *The Story of the Meininger*, trans. Ann Marie Koller, 1963
Osborne, J., *The Naturalist Drama in Germany*, 1971
Newmark, Maxim, *Otto Brahm: The Man and the Critic*, 1938

Gerhart Hauptmann
 — *The Dramatic Works*, trans. Ludwig Lewissohn, *et al.*, 1913—
 — *Five Plays*, trans. Theodore H. Lustig, 1961
Garten, Hugh F., *Gerhart Hauptmann*, 1954
Klemm, Frederick Alvin, *The Death Problem in the Life and Works of Gerhart Hauptmann*, 1939
Muller, S. H., *Gerhart Hauptmann and Goethe*, 1949
Sinden, Margaret, *Gerhart Hauptmann: The Prose Plays*, 1957
Stoeckius, Alfred, *Naturalism in the Recent German Drama, with Special Reference to Gerhart Hauptmann*, 1903

REALISM IN BRITAIN: THE NINETEENTH CENTURY AND AFTER

Agate, James, *Red Letter Nights*, 1944

Beerbohm, Max, *Around Theatres*, 1953

Borsa, Mario, *The English Stage of Today*, 1908

Carter, Huntly, *The New Spirit in Drama and Acting*, 1912

Chandler, F. W., *Aspects of Modern Drama*, 1914

Choudhuri, C., *Galsworthy's Plays: A Critical Survey*, 1961

Clark, Barrett H., *The British and American Drama of Today*, 1915
— *A Study of the Modern Drama*, 1928

Cook, Dutton, *The Book of the Play*, 1876
— *Nights at the Play*, 1883
— *On the Stage*, 1883

Darbyshire, A., *The Art of the Victorian Stage*, 1907

Dickinson, Thomas H., *The Contemporary Drama of England*, 1917

Dukes, Ashley, *Drama*, 1926
— *Modern Dramatists*, 1911
— *The World to Play with*, 1928
— *The Youngest Drama*, 1914

Dupont, V., *John Galsworthy: The Dramatic Artist*, 1946

George, W. L., *Dramatic Actualities*, 1914

Granville-Barker, Harley, *The Exemplary Theatre*, 1922
— *On Dramatic Method*, 1931
— *On Poetry in Drama*, 1937
— *The Study of Drama*, 1934
— *The Use of the Drama*, 1945

Hogan, Robert G., *Dion Boucicault*, 1969

Howe, P. P., *Dramatic Portraits*, 1913

James, Henry, *The Scenic Art: Notes on Acting and the Drama, 1872–1901*, 1948

Jones, Henry Arthur, *The Foundations of a National Drama*, 1913
— *The Renascence of the English Drama*, 1895

Lewissohn, Ludwig, *The Modern Drama*, 1915

MacCarthy, Desmond, *The Court Theatre, 1904–1907*, 1907
— *Theatre*, 1955

Montague, C. E., *Dramatic Values*, 1910

Nicoll, Allardyce, *English Drama, 1900–1930*, 1973
— *History of English Drama*, vol. v: *Late Nineteenth-Century Drama, 1850–1900*, 2nd edn, 1959

Palmer, John, *The Future of the Theatre*, 1913

Rowell, George, *The Victorian Theatre*, 2nd edn, 1979

Scott, Clement, *The Drama of Yesterday and To-day*, 2 vols., 1899

Sklar, S., *The Plays of D.H. Lawrence*, 1975

S[pence], E. F., *Our Stage and Its Critics*, 1910

Bibliography 189

Stokes, J., *Resistible Theatres: Enterprise and Experiment in the 19th Century*, 1972

Symons, Arthur, *Plays, Acting and Music*, 1903

Taylor, John Russell, *The Rise and Fall of the Well-Made Play*, 1967

Walkley, A. B., *Drama and Life*, 1908

— *Playhouse Impressions*, 1892

William Archer

— *About the Theatre*, 1886

— *English Dramatists of Today*, 1882

— 'Masks and Faces' in *The Paradox of Acting*, 1957

— *The Old Drama and the New*, 1923

— *Playmaking: A Manual of Craftsmanship*, 1912

— *Real Conversations*, 1907

— *Study and Stage*, 1899

— *The Theatrical World*, 5 vols., 1894–1898

Hamilton, Clayton, *Problems of the Playwright*, 1917

— *Studies in Stagecraft*, 1914

Matthews, Brander, 'A Critic of the Acted Drama: William Archer' in *The Historical Novel*, 1901

Shaw, George Bernard, Foreword to *Three Plays* by William Archer, 1927

J. T. Grein

— *Dramatic Criticism*, 5 vols., 1899–1905

— *The New World of the Theatre, 1923–1924*, 1924

— *Premiers of the Year May 1899–July 1900*, 1900

— *The World of the Theatre: Impressions and Memoirs, March 1920–1921*, 1921

Grein, Alix A., *J. T. Grein*, 1936

Schoonderwoerd, Nicolaas H. G., *J. T. Grein, Ambassador of the Theatre*, 1963

George Bernard Shaw

— *The Art of Rehearsal*, 1928

— *Bernard Shaw and Mrs Patrick Campbell: Their Correspondence*, 1952

— *Bernard Shaw's Letters to Granville-Barker*, ed. C. B. Purdom, 1956

— *Dramatic Opinions and Essays*, 2 vols., 1906

— *A Dramatic Realist to His Critics*, 1894

— *Ellen Terry and Bernard Shaw: A Correspondence*, 1931

— *Ibsen*, 1906

— *The New Drama*, 1911

— *Our Theatres in the Nineties*, 3 vols., 1932

— *Plays and Players: Essays on the Theatre*, ed. A. C. Ward, 1952

— Preface to *Three Plays* by Brieux, 1911

— Preface and Appendices to *Widowers' Houses* (Independent Theatre edn), 1893
— *Prefaces*, 1934
— *The Problem Play*, 1895
— *The Quintessence of Ibsenism*, 1891
— *Shaw's Dramatic Criticism, 1895–1898*, ed. J. H. Matthews, 1959
Bentley, Eric, *Bernard Shaw*, rev. edn, 1967
Berst, Charles A., *Bernard Shaw and the Art of Drama*, 1974
Bevan, E. D., *Concordance to the Plays and Prefaces of Bernard Shaw*, 1971
Burton, Richard, *Bernard Shaw, the Man and the Mask*, 1916
Chesterton, G. K., *George Bernard Shaw*, 1909
Collis, J. S., *Shaw*, 1925
Dukore, Bernard F., *Bernard Shaw, Director*, 1971
— *Bernard Shaw, Playwright: Aspects of Shavian Drama*, 1973
Ervine, St John, *Bernard Shaw: His Life, Work and Friends*, 1956
Evans, T. F., *Shaw: The Critical Heritage*, 1976
Hamon, Augustin, *The Twentieth Century Molière: Bernard Shaw*, trans. E. and C. Paul, 1916
Henderson, Archibald, *Bernard Shaw: Playboy and Prophet*, 1932
— *George Bernard Shaw: His Life and Works*, 1911
— *George Bernard Shaw: Man of the Century*, 1956
— *Table-Talk of G. B. S.*, 1925
Howe, P. P., *Bernard Shaw*, 1915
Irvine, William, *The Universe of G. B. S.*, 1949
Jackson, Holbrook, *Bernard Shaw*, 1907
Joad, C. E. M., *Shaw*, 1949
Kaufman, R. J., ed., *G. B. Shaw: A Collection of Critical Essays*, 1965
Kronenberger, Louis, ed., *Shaw: A Critical Survey*, 1953
MacCarthy, Desmond, *Shaw*, 1951
McCabe, Joseph, *George Bernard Shaw*, 1914
Mander, Raymond, and Mitchenson, Joe, *Theatrical Companion to Shaw*, 1955
Meisel, Martin, *Shaw and the Nineteenth-Century Theatre*, 1963
Mencken, H. L., *George Bernard Shaw, His Plays*, 1905
Mills, J. A., *Language and Laughter: Comic Diction in the Plays of Bernard Shaw*, 1969
Morgan, Margery M., *The Shavian Playground*, 1972
Nethercot, Arthur H., *Men and Supermen*, 1954
Ohmann, Richard M., *Shaw: The Style and the Man*, 1962
Palmer, John, *George Bernard Shaw, Harlequin or Patriot?*, 1915
Person, Hesketh, *G.B.S.: A Full Length Portrait*, 1942
— *G.B.S.: A Postscript*, 1950
Purdom, C. B., *A Guide to the Plays of Bernard Shaw*, 1963
Rattray, R. F., *Bernard Shaw: A Chronicle*, 1951
Shanks, Edward, *Bernard Shaw*, 1924

Valency, Maurice, *The Cart and the Trumpet*, 1973
Wall, Vincent, *Bernard Shaw: Pygmalion to Many Players*, 1973
West, Alick, *A Good Man Fallen among Fabians*, 1950
Whitman, Robert F., *Shaw and the Play of Ideas*, 1977
Woodbridge, Homer, *G. B. Shaw: Creative Artist*, 1963

REALISM IN RUSSIA: THE NINETEENTH CENTURY AND THE MOSCOW ART THEATRE

Bakshy, Alexander, *The Path of the Modern Russian Stage*, 1916
Fülop-Miller, Rene, and Gregor, Joseph, *The Russian Theatre*, 1930
Gorky, Maxim, *Reminiscences of Tolstoy, Chekhov and Andreyev*, trans.
        Katherine Mansfield, S. S., Koteliansky and Leonard Woolf, 1934
Kommisarjevsky, Theodore, *Myself and the Theatre*, 1930
Nemirovich-Danchenko, V., *My Life in the Russian Theatre*, trans. John
        Cournos, 1936
Sayler, Oliver M., *Inside the Moscow Art Theatre*, 1925
        — *The Russian Theatre under the Revolution*, 1920
Simmons, Ernest J., *An Outline of Modern Russian Literature (1880–1940)*,
        1943
Slonim, Marc, *Russian Theatre: From the Empire to the Soviets*, 1961
Weiner, Leo, *The Contemporary Drama of Russia*, 1924

Konstantin Stanislavsky

        — *Acting: A Handbook of the Stanislavsky Method*, ed. Toby Cole, 1947
        — *An Actor Prepares*, trans. Elizabeth Reynolds Hapgood, 1936
        — *An Actor's Handbook*, trans. Elizabeth Reynolds Hapgood, 1963
        — *Building a Character*, trans. Elizabeth Reynolds Hapgood, 1949
        — *Creating a Role*, trans. Elizabeth Reynolds Hapgood, 1961
        — *My Life in Art*, trans. J. J. Robbins, 1924
        — *The Seagull Produced by Stanislavsky*, 1952
        — *Stanislavsky on the Art of the Stage*, trans. David Magarshack, 1950
        — *Stanislavsky Produces Othello*, 1948
        — *Stanislavsky's Legacy*, ed. and trans. Elizabeth Reynolds Hapgood,
        1958
Chekhov, Michael A., *To the Actor: On the Technique of Acting*, 1953
        — *To the Director and Playwright*, ed. Charles Leonard, 1963
Edwards, Christine, *The Stanislavsky Heritage: Its Contribution to the
        Russian and American Theatre*, 1965
Freed, Donald, *Freud and Stanislavsky: New Direction in the Performing Arts*,
        1964
Gorchakov, Nikolai M., *Stanislavsky Directs*, trans. Miriam Goldina,
        1954
Lewis, Robert, *Method — or Madness?*, 1958
Magarshack, David, *Stanislavsky: A Life*, 1950
Marowitz, Charles, *The Method as Means*, 1961

— *Stanislavsky and the Method*, 1964
Moore, Sonia, *Training an Actor: The Stanislavsky System in Class*, 1968
Munk, Erika, ed., *Stanislavski and America*, 1966

Anton Chekhov
   — *Plays from the Russian*, trans. Constance Garnett, 1923
   — *Three Plays*, trans. Elisaveta Fen, 1951
   — *The Seagull and Other Plays*, trans. Elisaveta Fen, 1954
   — *Six Plays of Chekhov*, trans. Robert W. Corrigan, 1962
   — *The Oxford Chekhov*, trans. Ronald Hingley, 3 vols., 1964–8

   — *Letters of Anton Chekhov to His Family and Friends*, trans. Constance
      Garnett, 1920
   — *Letters on the Short Story, the Drama, and Other Literary Topics*, ed.
      Louis S. Friedland, 1924
   — *The Life and Letters of Anton Tchekhov*, trans. S. S. Koteliansky and
      Philip Tomlinson, 1925
   — *The Selected Letters*, ed. Lillian Hellman and trans. Sidonie Lederer,
      1955
   — *Letters of Anton Chekhov*, ed. Avrahm Yarmolinsky, 1973

Brahms, Caryl, *Reflections in a Lake: A Study of Chekhov's Four Greatest
      Plays*, 1976
Bruford, W. H., *Chekhov*, 1957
   — *Chekhov and His Russia*, 1947
Garnett, Edward, *Chekhov and His Art*, 1929
Gerhardi, William, *Anton Chekhov: A Critical Study*, 1923
Hahn, Beverly, *Chekhov: A Study of the Major Stories and Plays*, 1977
Hingley, Ronald, *Chekhov: A Biographical and Critical Study*, 1950
   — *A New Life of Anton Chekhov*, 1976
Koteliansky, S. S., ed., *Anton Chekhov: Literary and Theatrical Reminiscences*,
      1927
Laffitte, Sophie, *Chekhov: 1860–1904*, trans. Moura Budberg and Gordon
      Latta, 1973
Magarshack, David, *Chekhov: A Life*, 1952
   — *Chekhov the Dramatist*, 1952
   — *The Real Chekhov*, 1972
Pitcher, Harvey, *The Chekhov Play: A New Interpretation*, 1973
Simmons, Ernest J., *Chekhov: A Biography*, 1962
Styan, J. L., *Chekhov in Performance: A Commentary on the Major Plays*,
      1971
Toumanova, N. N., *Anton Chekhov, the Voice of Twilight Russia*, 1937
Valency, Maurice, *The Breaking String: The Plays of Anton Chekhov*, 1966

Maxim Gorky
   — *Five Plays*, trans. Margaret Wettlin, 1959
   — *The Last Plays of Maxim Gorky*, trans. W. L. Gibson-Cowan, 1937

— *Seven Plays*, trans. Alexander Bakshy and Paul S. Nathan, 1945
— *The Lower Depths and Other Plays*, trans. Alexander Bakshy and Paul S. Nathan, 1959
— *The Lower Depths*, trans. Alexander Bakshy, 1961, Moura Budberg, 1959, Jennie Covan, 1923, Kitty Hunter-Blair and Jeremy Brooks, 1973, Laurence Irving, 1912
— *The Storm and Other Russian Plays*, trans. David Magarshack, 1960

— *Autobiography*, trans. Isidor Schneider, 1953
— *My Apprenticeship*, trans. Ronald Wilks, 1974
— *Letters*, trans. V. Dutt, ed. P. Cockerell, 1966
— *Letters of Gorky and Andreev, 1899—1912*, trans. Lydia Weston, ed. Peter Yershov, 1958.
— *The Letters to V. F. Xodasević, 1922—5*, trans. Hugh McLean, 1953

von Dillon, E. J., *Maxim Gorky: His Life and Writings*, 1902
Habermann, Gerhard E. E., *Maksim Gorki*, trans. Ernestine Schlaut, 1971
Hare, Richard, *Maxim Gorky, Romantic Realist and Conservative Revolutionary*, 1962
Holtzmann, Filia, *The Young Maxim Gorky, 1868—1902*, 1948
Kaun, A. S., *Maxim Gorky and His Russia*, 1932
Levin, Dan, *Stormy Petrel: The Life and Work of Maxim Gorky*, 1967
Muchnic, Helen, *From Gorky to Pasternak: Six Writers in Soviet Russia*, 1961
Olgin, M. I., *Maxim Gorky, Writer and Revolutionist*, 1933

THE IRISH DRAMATIC MOVEMENT
(*see also* vols. 2 and 3)

Byrne, Dawson, *The Story of Ireland's National Theatre, the Abbey*, 1929
Ellis-Fermor, Una, *The Irish Dramatic Movement*, rev. edn, 1954
Fay, Gerard, *The Abbey Theatre, Cradle of Genius*, 1958
Fay, W. G., *Merely Players*, 1932
    and Carswell, Catharine, *The Fays of the Abbey Theatre*, 1935
Gregory, Lady, *Journals, 1916—1930*, ed. Lennox Robinson, 1947
    — *Our Irish Theatre*, 1913
    — *Seventy Years. Being the Autobiography of Lady Gregory*, ed. Colin Smythe, 1976
Hogan, Robert G., *After the Irish Renaissance: A Critical History of the Irish Drama since 'The Plough and the Stars'*, 1967
    and Kilroy, James, *The Modern Irish Drama*, vols. 1—3, 1975—8
    and O'Neill, Michael J., eds., *Joseph Holloway's Abbey Theatre*, 1967
    — *Joseph Holloway's Irish Theatre*, 1970.
Kavanagh, Peter, *The Irish Theatre*, 1946
    — *The Story of the Abbey Theatre*, 1950
MacLiammoir, Michael, *All for Hecuba: An Irish Theatrical Autobiography*, 1946

Malone, A. E., *The Irish Drama*, 1929
Mikhail, E. H., *A Bibliography of Modern Irish Drama, 1899—1970,* 1972
Moore, George, *Hail and Farewell,* 3 vols., 1911—13
NicShiubhlaigh Máire, and Kenny, Edward, *The Splendid Years,* 1955
Robinson, Lennox, *Ireland's Abbey Theatre: A History, 1899—1951,* 1951
    — ed., *The Irish Theatre,* 1939
Weygandt, Cornelius, *Irish Plays and Players,* 1913

John Millington Synge
Bickley, Francis L., *J. M. Synge and the Irish Dramatic Movement,* 1912
Bourgeois, Maurice, *John Millington Synge and the Irish Theatre,* 1913
Corkery, Daniel, *Synge and Anglo-Irish Literature,* 1965
Estill, Adelaide Duncan, *The Sources of Synge,* 1939
Greene, David H., and Stephens, Edward M., *John Millington Synge, 1871—
    1909,* 1959
Henn, T. R., ed., Introductions to *The Plays and Poems of J. M. Synge,* 1963
Howe, P. P., *J. M. Synge,* 1912
Masefield, John, *John M. Synge: A Few Personal Recollections,* 1916
Mikhail, E. H., ed., *J. M. Synge: Interviews and Recollections,* 1977
Murphy, Daniel J., 'The Reception of Synge's *Playboy* in Ireland and
    America: 1907—1912', *Bulletin of the New York Public Library,*
    vol. 64, 1960
Price, Alan, *Synge and Anglo-Irish Drama,* 1961
Strong, L. A. G., *John Millington Synge,* 1941
Yeats, W. B., *John Millington Synge and the Ireland of His Time,* 1911

Sean O'Casey
    — *Autobiographies,* 2 vols., 1963
    — *Autobiography,* 6 vols., 1939—54
    — *Feathers from the Green Crow: Sean O'Casey, 1905—1925,* ed. Robert
    G. Hogan, 1962
    — *The Flying Wasp: A Laughing Look over, etc,* 1937
    — *The Green Crow* [Essays and Short Stories], 1957

Armstrong, William A., *Sean O'Casey,* 1967
Ayling, R., *Sean O'Casey,* 1969
Cowasjee, Saros, *O'Casey,* 1966
Hogan, Robert G., *The Experiments of Sean O'Casey,* 1960
Koslow, Jules, *The Green and the Red: Sean O'Casey, the Man and His Plays,*
    1949, rev. edn., 1966
Krause, David, *Sean O'Casey: The Man and His Work,* 1960
MacCann, Sean, *The World of Sean O'Casey,* 1966
Malone, Maureen, *The Plays of Sean O'Casey,* 1969
O'Casey, Eileen, *Sean,* 1971
Rollins, Ronald Gene, *Sean O'Casey's Drama: Verisimilitude and Vision,*
    1978

REALISM IN AMERICA
(*See also* vol. 3)

Abramson, Doris E., *Negro Playwrights in the American Theatre, 1925–1959*, 1969

Anderson, John, *The American Theater*, 1938
— *Box Office*, 1929

Atkinson, Brooks, *Broadway Scrapbook*, 1947

Baker, George Pierce, *Dramatic Technique*, 1919

Belasco, David, *The Theatre through Its Stage Door*, 1919

Bentley, Eric, *The Dramatic Event: An American Chronicle*, 1954

Bigsby, C.W.E., *Confrontation and Commitment: A Study of Contemporary American Drama, 1959–1966*, 1967

Blau, Herbert, *The Impossible Theatre: A Manifesto*, 1964

Block, Anita, *The Changing World in Plays and Theatre*, 1939

Brown, John Mason, *The American Theatre As Seen by Its Critics, 1752–1934*, 1934
— *Broadway in Review*, 1940
— *Letters from Greenroom Ghosts*, 1934
— *Seeing Things*, 1946
— *Two on the Aisle*, 1938
— *Upstage*, 1930

Cheney, Sheldon, *The Art Theater*, 1925
— *The New Movement in the Theater*, 1914

Clark, Barrett H., *A Study of the Modern Drama*, 1938
— *An Hour of American Drama*, 1930

Clurman, Harold, *The Fervent Years: The Story of the Group Theatre and the Thirties*, 1945
— *Lies like Truth*, 1958
— *The Naked Image*, 1966

Cohn, Ruby, *Dialogue in American Drama*, 1971

Deutsch, Helen, and Hanau, Stella, *The Provincetown*, 1931

Dickinson, Thomas H., *The Case of American Drama*, 1915
— *The Insurgent Theater*, 1917
— *Playwrights of the New American Theater*, 1925

Downer, Alan S., ed., *American Drama and Its Critics*, 1965
— *Fifty Years of American Drama, 1900–1950*, 1951

Eaton, Walter Prichard, ed., *The Theatre Guild: The First Ten Years*, 1929

Flanagan, Hallie, *Arena: The History of the Federal Theatre*, 1965

Flexner, Eleanor, *American Playwrights, 1918–1938*, 1938

Frick, Constance, *The Dramatic Criticism of George Jean Nathan*, 1943

Gassner, John, *Theatre at the Crossroads*, 1960
— *The Theatre in Our Time*, 1954

Gorelik Mordecai, *New Theatres for Old*, 1940

Gould, Jean, *Modern American Playwrights*, 1966

Green Paul, *Drama and the Weather*, 1958

— *Dramatic Heritage*, 1953
— *The Hawthorn Tree*, 1943
Hellman, Lillian, Introduction to *Four Plays*, 1942
Hewitt, Barnard, *Theater USA, 1668–1957*, 1958
Hughes, Catherine, *American Playwrights, 1945–1975*, 1976
Inge, William, Foreword to *Four Plays*, 1958
Jones, Robert Edmond, *The Dramatic Imagination: Reflections and Speculations on the Art of the Theatre*, 1941
Kaufman, S., *Persons of the Drama: Theatre Criticism and Comment*, 1976
Kerr, Walter, *How Not to Write a Play*, 1955
— *Pieces at Eight*, 1957
— *The Theater in Spite of Itself*, 1963
Kinne, Wisner Payne, *George Pierce Baker and the American Theatre*, 1954
Krutch, Joseph Wood, *The American Drama since 1918*, rev. edn, 1957
Lahr, John, *Astonish Me: Adventures in Contemporary Theater*, 1973
Macgowan, Kenneth, *A Primer of Playwriting*, 1921
— *The Theater of Tomorrow*, 1921
— and Jones, Robert Edmond, *Continental Stagecraft*, 1922
McCarthy, Mary, *Sights and Spectacles*, 1956
— *Theatre Chronicles, 1937–1962*, 1963
McCullers, Carson, 'The Vision Shared' in *Theatre Arts*, April 1950
Mantle, Burns, *American Playwrights of Today*, 1938
Marker, Lise-Lone, *David Belasco: Naturalism in the American Theatre*, 1975
Matthews, Brander, *On Acting*, 1914
— *Rip Van Winkle Goes to the Play*, 1926
Mielziner, Jo, *Designing for the Theatre*, 1965
Moody, Richard, *Lillian Hellman, Playwright*, 1972
Moses, Montrose J., *The American Dramatist*, 1925
— and Brown, John Mason, eds., *The American Theatre as Seen by Its Critics*, 1934
Motherwell, Hiram H., *The Theater of Today*, 1914
Nathan, George Jean, *Another Book on the Theatre*, 1915
— *Art of the Night*, 1928
— *Passing Judgments*, 1935
Novick, Julius, *Beyond Broadway*, 1968
O'Connor, John and Lorraine, Browne, eds., *Free, Adult, Uncensored: The Living History of the Federal Theatre Project*, 1978
Odell, George C. D., *Annals of the New York Stage*, 15 vols., 1927–49
O'Hara, Frank Hurlburt, *Today in American Drama*, 1939
Pendleton, Ralph, ed., *The Theatre of Robert Edmond Jones*, 1958
Poggi, James, *Theatre in America: The Impact of Economic Forces, 1870–1967*, 1968
Porter, Thomas E., *Myth and Modern American Drama*, 1969

Rabkin, Gerald, *Drama and Commitment: Politics in the American Theatre of the Thirties*, 1964
Rice, Elmer, *The Living Theatre*, 1959
  — Introduction to *Two Plays*, 1935
Sayler, Oliver M., *Our American Theater*, 1923
Sievers, W. David, *Freud on Broadway*, 1955
Simonson, Lee, *The Stage Is Set*, 1932
Strasberg, Lee, *Strasberg at the Actors' Studio*, ed. R. E. Hethman, 1965
Waldau, R. S., *Vintage Years of the Theatre Guild, 1928–1939*, 1972
Weales, Gerald, *American Drama since World War II*, 1962
  — *The Jumping Off Place: American Drama in the Sixties*, 1969
Wilder, Thornton, Preface to *Three Plays*, 1957
Winter, William, *The Life of David Belasco*, 2 vols., 1925
Woollcott, Alexander, *Enchanted Isles*, 1924
  — *Going to Pieces*, 1928
  — *Shouts and Murmurs*, 1922
Young, Stark, *The Flower in Drama: A Book of Papers on the Theatre*, 1923
  — *Immortal Shadows: A Book of Dramatic Criticism*, 1948

Tennessee Williams
  — *Forewords to individual plays*

Donahue, Francis, *The Dramatic World of Tennessee Williams*, 1964
Falk, Signi L., *Tennesseee Williams*, 1961
Hurrell, John D., ed., *Two Modern American Tragedies: Reviews and Criticism of 'Death of a Salesman' and 'A Streetcar Named Desire'*, 1961
Jackson, Esther, *The Broken World of Tennessee Williams*, 1965
Nelson, Benjamin, *Tennessee Williams: The Man and His Work*, 1961
Tischler, Nancy M., *Tennessee Williams, Rebellious Puritan*, 1961
Weales, Gerald C., *Tennessee Williams*, 1965
Williams, Edwina Dakin, *Remember Me to Tom*, 1963

Arthur Miller
  — Introduction to *Collected Plays*, 1957
  — *The Theater Essays of Arthur Miller*, ed. Robert A. Martin, 1978

Corrigan, Robert W., *Arthur Miller: A Collection of Critical Essays*, 1969
Hayashi, Tetsumaro, *Arthur Miller Criticism, 1930–1967*, 1969
Hayman, Ronald, *Arthur Miller*, 1972
Hogan, Robert G., *Arthur Miller*, 1964
Huftel, Sheila, *Arthur Miller: The Burning Glass*, 1965
Hurrell, John D., ed., *Two Modern American Tragedies: Reviews and Criticism of 'Death of a Salesman' and 'A Streetcar Named Desire'*, 1961
Moss, Leonard, *Arthur Miller*, 1967
Welland, Dennis, *Arthur Miller*, 1961

REALISM IN BRITAIN, THE FIRST WORLD WAR TO THE PRESENT

(See also vols. 2 and 3)

Agate, James, *The Contemporary Theatre, 1923—1926*, 4 vols., 1924—7
   — *First Nights*, 1934
   — *More First Nights*, 1937
   — *A Short View of the English Stage*, 1926
Anderson, Michael, *Anger and Detachment: A Study of Arden, Osborne and Pinter*, 1976
Armstrong, W. A., ed., *Experimental Drama*, 1963
Bishop, G. W., *Barry Jackson and the London Theatre*, 1933
Brown, Ivor, *Masques and Faces*, 1926
   — *Parties of the Play*, 1928
Brown, John Russell, *Theatre Language: A Study of Arden, Osborne, Pinter and Wester*, 1972
   and Harris, Bernard, eds., *Contemporary Theatre*, 1962
Browne, Terry, *Playwrights' Theatre: The English Stage Company at the Royal Court Theatre*, 1975
Cunliffe, J. W., *Modern English Playwrights*, 1927
Darlington, W. A., *Six Thousand and One Nights: Forty Years a Critic*, 1960
Evans, Gareth Lloyd, *The Language of Modern Drama*, 1977
Gielgud, John, *Early Stages*, 1939
   — *Stage Directions*, 1963
Goodwin, John, ed., *The Royal Shakespeare Company, 1960—1963*, 1964
Guthrie, Tyrone, *A Life in the Theatre*, 1959
   — *A New Theatre*, 1964
   — *Theatre Prospect*, 1932
Hayman, Ronald, *Arnold Wesker*, 2nd edn, 1974
   — *John Osborne*, 2nd edn, 1970
   — *The Set-up: An Anatomy of the English Theatre Today*, 1973
Hinchliffe, Arnold, *The British Theatre, 1950—1970*, 1974
Hobson, Harold, *Verdict at Midnight*, 1952
Kitchin, Laurence, *Mid-Century Drama*, 1960
Leeming, G. and Trussler, S., *The Plays of Arnold Wesker: An Assessment*, 1971
Marowitz, Charles, and Trussler, Simon, eds., *Theatre at Work: Playwrights and Productions in the Modern British Theatre*, 1967
   — and Milne, Tom and Hale, Owen, eds., *The Encore Reader: A Chronicle of the New Drama*, 1965
Peacock, Ronald, *The Poet in the Theatre*, 1946, rev. edn, 1960
Playfair, Nigel, *The Story of the Lyric Theatre, Hammersmith*, 1925
Popkin, Henry, *The New British Drama*, 1964
Redgrave, Michael, *The Actor's Ways and Means*, 1954
Reynolds, Ernest, *Modern English Drama*, 1949
Sutton, Graham, *Some Contemporary Dramatists*, 1926

Taylor, John Russell, *Anger and After: A Guide to the New British Drama*, 1962
 — *The Second Wave: British Drama of the Sixties*, 1971, rev. edn, 1978
Trewin, J. C., *The Birmingham Repertory Theatre, 1913–1963*, 1963
Tynan, Kenneth, *Curtains*, 1961
 — *He That Plays the King*, 1950
Wardle, Irving, *The Theatres of George Devine*, 1978
Wickham, Glynne, *Drama in a World of Science*, 1962
Worsley, T. C., *The Fugitive Art*, 1952

Index